WILLIAM
SHAKESPEARE

OTHELLO

CLASSICS

Published 2024

FiNGERPRINT! CLASSICS
Prakash Books

 Fingerprint Publishing
 @FingerprintP
 @fingerprintpublishingbooks
www.fingerprintpublishing.com

ISBN: 978 93 8917 849 4

William Shakespeare began his career as an actor, writer, and part owner of a playing company called the Lord Chamberlain's Men, later known as King's Men, in London. Often regarded as the 'Bard of Avon' he is one of the world's pre-eminent dramatists. Born and brought up in Stratford-upon-Avon, he married Anne Hathaway at the age of eighteen and they had three children—Susanna, and twins Hamnet and Judith. Though few records survive of his private life, he appeared to have retired to Stratford around 1613 where he died three years later.

His works still in existence, including some collaborations, consist of thirty-eight plays, one hundred and fifty-four sonnets, two long narrative poems, and several other verses. His plays are performed much more than any other playwright's and have been translated in almost all major languages. Most of his known works have been produced between 1589 and 1613. His early plays were mainly comedies and histories which remain regarded as some of the best works produced in these genres.

Shakespeare's plays are difficult to date. His early classical and Italianate comedies contain tight double plots and precise comic sequences giving way to the romantic atmosphere of his most acclaimed comedies in the mid-1590s. *A Midsummer Night's Dream*—a witty mixture of romance, fairy magic, and comic low life scenes—is one of his most delightful creations shortly before he turned to *Romeo and Juliet*. *Romeo and Juliet* is his most famous romantic tragedy of sexually charged adolescence, love, and death. It marks a departure from his earlier works and from others of the English Renaissance.

His plays demonstrate the expansiveness of his imagination and the extent of his learning. Shakespeare's sequence of great comedies continues with *Merchant of Venice*, *Much Ado About Nothing*, *As You Like It*, and *Twelfth Night*. One of his best-loved comedies, *Twelfth Night* is a romantic drama of confusions, comic sequences, and mistaken identities.

Shakespeare introduced prose comedy in the histories of the late 1590s—*Henry IV, Part I* and *Part II, and Henry V*—after the lyrical *Richard II*. *Julius Caesar* introduced a new kind of drama. Based on true events from Roman history, it is one of Shakespeare's most loved political tragedies.

Shakespeare wrote the so-called 'problem plays' in the early 17th century. *Measure for*

Measure, Troilus and Cressida, and *All's Well that Ends Well* being a few of them. Until about 1608, he mainly wrote tragedies including *Hamlet, Othello, King Lear,* and *Macbeth.*

Othello is the story of the eponymous character who is a soldier in the service of the Venetian Republic. On instigation of his villainous ensign, Iago, Othello murders his beloved wife, Desdemona, only to find out later that she is innocent. An emotional drama of love, jealously, betrayal, revenge, and repentance, *Othello* reveals how fabricated lies and manipulation of evidences can lead to wrong judgement and suddenness of action, which ultimately result in the fall of a man.

Antony and Cleopatra and *Coriolanus*—his last major tragedies, contain some of his finest poetry. Shakespeare wrote tragicomedies, also known as romances, in his last phase. These include *Cymbeline, The Winter's Tale,* and *The Tempest,* as well as the collaboration *Pericles, Prince of Tyre.*

A true genius, Shakespeare's popular characters and plots are studied, performed, reinterpreted, and discussed till today. William Shakespeare, known as the English national poet, is considered the greatest dramatist of all time.

CHARACTERS OF THE PLAY

OTHELLO, the Moor, general of the Venetian forces

DESDEMONA, his wife

IAGO, ensign to Othello

EMILIA, his wife, lady-in-waiting to Desdemona

CASSIO, lieutenant to Othello

DUKE OF VENICE

BRABANTIO, Venetian Senator, father of Desdemona

GRATIANO, nobleman of Venice, brother of Brabantio

LODOVICO, nobleman of Venice, kinsman of Brabantio

RODERIGO, rejected suitor of Desdemona

BIANCA, mistress of Cassio

MONTANO, a Cypriot official
CLOWN, a servant to Othello
Senators, Sailors, Messengers, Officers, Gentlemen,
Musicians, and Attendants

SCENE:
VENICE AND CYPRUS

Act I

SCENE I. VENICE. A STREET.

Enter RODERIGO and IAGO

RODERIGO

    Tush! never tell me; I take it much unkindly

    That thou, Iago, who hast had my purse

    As if the strings were thine, shouldst know of
        this.

IAGO

    'Sblood, but you will not hear me:

    If ever I did dream of such a matter, Abhor me.

RODERIGO

    Thou told'st me thou didst hold him in thy
    hate.

IAGO

    Despise me, if I do not. Three great ones of
        the city,

In personal suit to make me his lieutenant,
Off-capp'd to him: and, by the faith of man,
I know my price, I am worth no worse a place:
But he; as loving his own pride and purposes,
Evades them, with a bombast circumstance
Horribly stuff'd with epithets of war;
And, in conclusion,
Nonsuits my mediators; for, 'Certes,' says he,
'I have already chose my officer.'
And what was he?
Forsooth, a great arithmetician,
One Michael Cassio, a Florentine,
A fellow almost damn'd in a fair wife;
That never set a squadron in the field,
Nor the division of a battle knows
More than a spinster; unless the bookish theoric,
Wherein the toged consuls can propose
As masterly as he: mere prattle, without practise,
Is all his soldiership. But he, sir, had the election:
And I, of whom his eyes had seen the proof
At Rhodes, at Cyprus and on other grounds
Christian and heathen, must be be-lee'd and
     calm'd
By debitor and creditor: this counter-caster,
He, in good time, must his lieutenant be,
And I—God bless the mark!—his Moorship's
     ancient.

RODERIGO

By heaven, I rather would have been his hangman.

IAGO

Why, there's no remedy; 'tis the curse of service,
Preferment goes by letter and affection,
And not by old gradation, where each second
Stood heir to the first. Now, sir, be judge yourself,
Whether I in any just term am affined
To love the Moor.

RODERIGO

I would not follow him then.

IAGO

O, sir, content you;
I follow him to serve my turn upon him:
We cannot all be masters, nor all masters
Cannot be truly follow'd. You shall mark
Many a duteous and knee-crooking knave,
That, doting on his own obsequious bondage,
Wears out his time, much like his master's ass,
For nought but provender, and when he's old, cashier'd:
Whip me such honest knaves. Others there are
Who, trimm'd in forms and visages of duty,
Keep yet their hearts attending on themselves,
And, throwing but shows of service on their lords,

13

Do well thrive by them and when they have
    lined their coats
Do themselves homage: these fellows have
    some soul;
And such a one do I profess myself. For, sir,
It is as sure as you are Roderigo,
Were I the Moor, I would not be Iago:
In following him, I follow but myself;
Heaven is my judge, not I for love and duty,
But seeming so, for my peculiar end:
For when my outward action doth demonstrate
The native act and figure of my heart
In compliment extern, 'tis not long after
But I will wear my heart upon my sleeve
For daws to peck at: I am not what I am.

RODERIGO

What a full fortune does the thick-lips owe
If he can carry't thus!

IAGO

Call up her father,
Rouse him: make after him, poison his delight,
Proclaim him in the streets; incense her
    kinsmen,
And, though he in a fertile climate dwell,
Plague him with flies: though that his joy be joy,
Yet throw such changes of vexation on't,
As it may lose some colour.

RODERIGO

Here is her father's house; I'll call aloud.

IAGO

Do, with like timorous accent and dire yell
As when, by night and negligence, the fire
Is spied in populous cities.

RODERIGO

What, ho, Brabantio! Signior Brabantio, ho!

IAGO

Awake! what, ho, Brabantio! thieves! thieves!
thieves!
Look to your house, your daughter and your
bags!
Thieves! thieves!

BRABANTIO appears above, at a window

BRABANTIO

What is the reason of this terrible summons?
What is the matter there?

RODERIGO

Signior, is all your family within?

IAGO

Are your doors lock'd?

BRABANTIO

Why, wherefore ask you this?

IAGO

Zounds, sir, you're robb'd; for shame, put on
your gown;

Your heart is burst, you have lost half your soul;
Even now, now, very now, an old black ram
Is tupping your white ewe. Arise, arise;
Awake the snorting citizens with the bell,
Or else the devil will make a grandsire of you:
Arise, I say.

BRABANTIO

What, have you lost your wits?

RODERIGO

Most reverend signior, do you know my voice?

BRABANTIO

Not I what are you?

RODERIGO

My name is Roderigo.

BRABANTIO

The worser welcome:
I have charged thee not to haunt about my
    doors:
In honest plainness thou hast heard me say
My daughter is not for thee; and now, in
    madness,
Being full of supper and distempering draughts,
Upon malicious bravery, dost thou come
To start my quiet.

RODERIGO

Sir, sir, sir—

BRABANTIO

But thou must needs be sure
My spirit and my place have in them power
To make this bitter to thee.

RODERIGO

Patience, good sir.

BRABANTIO

What tell'st thou me of robbing? This is Venice;
My house is not a grange.

RODERIGO

Most grave Brabantio,
In simple and pure soul I come to you.

IAGO

Zounds, sir, you are one of those that will not
serve God, if the devil bid you. Because we
come to do you service and you think we are
ruffians, you'll have your daughter covered
with a Barbary horse; you'll have your nephews
neigh to you; you'll have coursers for cousins
and gennets for germans.

BRABANTIO

What profane wretch art thou?

IAGO

I am one, sir, that comes to tell you your
daughter and the Moor are now making the
beast with two backs.

BRABANTIO

Thou art a villain.

IAGO

You are—a senator.

BRABANTIO

This thou shalt answer; I know thee, Roderigo.

RODERIGO

Sir, I will answer any thing. But, I beseech you,
If't be your pleasure and most wise consent,
As partly I find it is, that your fair daughter,
At this odd-even and dull watch o' the night,
Transported, with no worse nor better guard
But with a knave of common hire, a gondolier,
To the gross clasps of a lascivious Moor—
If this be known to you and your allowance,
We then have done you bold and saucy wrongs;
But if you know not this, my manners tell me
We have your wrong rebuke. Do not believe
That, from the sense of all civility,
I thus would play and trifle with your reverence:
Your daughter, if you have not given her leave,
I say again, hath made a gross revolt;
Tying her duty, beauty, wit and fortunes
In an extravagant and wheeling stranger
Of here and every where. Straight satisfy
    yourself:
If she be in her chamber or your house,

Let loose on me the justice of the state
For thus deluding you.

BRABANTIO

Strike on the tinder, ho!
Give me a taper! call up all my people!
This accident is not unlike my dream:
Belief of it oppresses me already.
Light, I say! light!

Exit above

IAGO

Farewell; for I must leave you:
It seems not meet, nor wholesome to my place,
To be produced—as, if I stay, I shall—
Against the Moor: for, I do know, the state,
However this may gall him with some check,
Cannot with safety cast him, for he's embark'd
With such loud reason to the Cyprus wars,
Which even now stand in act, that, for their
    souls,
Another of his fathom they have none,
To lead their business: in which regard,
Though I do hate him as I do hell-pains.
Yet, for necessity of present life,
I must show out a flag and sign of love,
Which is indeed but sign. That you shall surely
    find him,
Lead to the Sagittary the raised search;

And there will I be with him. So, farewell.

Exit

Enter, below, BRABANTIO, and
Servants with torches

BRABANTIO

    It is too true an evil: gone she is;

    And what's to come of my despised time

    Is nought but bitterness. Now, Roderigo,

    Where didst thou see her? O unhappy girl!

    With the Moor, say'st thou? Who would be a
       father!

    How didst thou know 'twas she? O she deceives
       me

    Past thought! What said she to you? Get more
       tapers:

    Raise all my kindred. Are they married, think
       you?

RODERIGO

    Truly, I think they are.

BRABANTIO

    O heaven! How got she out? O treason of the
       blood!

    Fathers, from hence trust not your daughters'
       minds

    By what you see them act. Is there not charms

    By which the property of youth and maidhood

May be abused? Have you not read, Roderigo,
Of some such thing?

RODERIGO

Yes, sir, I have indeed.

BRABANTIO

Call up my brother. O, would you had had her!
Some one way, some another. Do you know
Where we may apprehend her and the Moor?

RODERIGO

I think I can discover him, if you please,
To get good guard and go along with me.

BRABANTIO

Pray you, lead on. At every house I'll call;
I may command at most. Get weapons, ho!
And raise some special officers of night.
On, good Roderigo: I'll deserve your pains.

Exeunt

SCENE II. ANOTHER STREET

Enter OTHELLO, IAGO, and Attendants with torches

IAGO

Though in the trade of war I have slain men,
Yet do I hold it very stuff o' the conscience
To do no contrived murder: I lack iniquity
Sometimes to do me service: nine or ten times

I had thought to have yerk'd him here under
the ribs.

OTHELLO

'Tis better as it is.

IAGO

Nay, but he prated,
And spoke such scurvy and provoking terms
Against your honour
That, with the little godliness I have,
I did full hard forbear him. But, I pray you, sir,
Are you fast married? Be assured of this,
That the magnifico is much beloved,
And hath in his effect a voice potential
As double as the Duke's: he will divorce you;
Or put upon you what restraint and grievance
The law, with all his might to enforce it on,
Will give him cable.

OTHELLO

Let him do his spite:
My services which I have done the signiory
Shall out-tongue his complaints. 'Tis yet to
know—
Which, when I know that boasting is an honour,
I shall promulgate—I fetch my life and being
From men of royal siege, and my demerits
May speak unbonneted to as proud a fortune
As this that I have reach'd: for know, Iago,

But that I love the gentle Desdemona,
I would not my unhoused free condition
Put into circumscription and confine
For the sea's worth. But, look! what lights come
    yond?

IAGO

Those are the raised father and his friends:
You were best go in.

OTHELLO

Not I I must be found:
My parts, my title and my perfect soul
Shall manifest me rightly. Is it they?

IAGO

By Janus, I think no.
Enter CASSIO, and certain Officers with torches

OTHELLO

The servants of the Duke, and my lieutenant.
The goodness of the night upon you, friends!
What is the news?

CASSIO

The Duke does greet you, general,
And he requires your haste-post-haste
    appearance,
Even on the instant.

OTHELLO

What is the matter, think you?

CASSIO

Something from Cyprus as I may divine:
It is a business of some heat: the galleys
Have sent a dozen sequent messengers
This very night at one another's heels,
And many of the consuls, raised and met,
Are at the Duke's already: you have been hotly
     call'd for;
When, being not at your lodging to be found,
The Senate hath sent about three several quests
To search you out.

OTHELLO

'Tis well I am found by you.
I will but spend a word here in the house,
And go with you.

Exit

CASSIO

Ancient, what makes he here?

IAGO

Faith, he to-night hath boarded a land carrack:
If it prove lawful prize, he's made for ever.

CASSIO

I do not understand.

IAGO

He's married.

CASSIO

To who?

Re-enter OTHELLO

IAGO

Marry, to—Come, captain, will you go?

OTHELLO

Have with you.

CASSIO

Here comes another troop to seek for you.

IAGO

It is Brabantio. General, be advised;

He comes to bad intent.

Enter BRABANTIO, RODERIGO, and
Officers with torches and weapons

OTHELLO

Holla! stand there!

RODERIGO

Signior, it is the Moor.

BRABANTIO

Down with him, thief!

They draw on both sides

IAGO

You, Roderigo! come, sir, I am for you.

OTHELLO

Keep up your bright swords, for the dew will
rust them.

Good signior, you shall more command with
years

Than with your weapons.

BRABANTIO

> O thou foul thief, where hast thou stow'd my
>   daughter?
> Damn'd as thou art, thou hast enchanted her;
> For I'll refer me to all things of sense,
> If she in chains of magic were not bound,
> Whether a maid so tender, fair and happy,
> So opposite to marriage that she shunned
> The wealthy curled darlings of our nation,
> Would ever have, to incur a general mock,
> Run from her guardage to the sooty bosom
> Of such a thing as thou, to fear, not to delight.
> Judge me the world, if 'tis not gross in sense
> That thou hast practised on her with foul
>   charms,
> Abused her delicate youth with drugs or minerals
> That weaken motion: I'll have't disputed on;
> 'Tis probable and palpable to thinking.
> I therefore apprehend and do attach thee
> For an abuser of the world, a practiser
> Of arts inhibited and out of warrant.
> Lay hold upon him: if he do resist,
> Subdue him at his peril.

OTHELLO

> Hold your hands,
> Both you of my inclining, and the rest:
> Were it my cue to fight, I should have known it

Without a prompter. Where will you that I go
To answer this your charge?

BRABANTIO

To prison, till fit time
Of law and course of direct session
Call thee to answer.

OTHELLO

What if I do obey?
How may the Duke be therewith satisfied,
Whose messengers are here about my side,
Upon some present business of the state
To bring me to him?

FIRST OFFICER

'Tis true, most worthy signior;
The Duke's in council and your noble self,
I am sure, is sent for.

BRABANTIO

How! The Duke in council!
In this time of the night! Bring him away:
Mine's not an idle cause: the Duke himself,
Or any of my brothers of the state,
Cannot but feel this wrong as 'twere their own;
For if such actions may have passage free,
Bond-slaves and pagans shall our statesmen be.

Exeunt

SCENE III. A COUNCIL-CHAMBER

The DUKE and Senators sitting at a table; Officers attending

DUKE OF VENICE

    There is no composition in these news

    That gives them credit.

FIRST SENATOR

    Indeed, they are disproportion'd;

    My letters say a hundred and seven galleys.

DUKE OF VENICE

    And mine, a hundred and forty.

SECOND SENATOR

    And mine, two hundred:

    But though they jump not on a just account—

    As in these cases, where the aim reports,

    'Tis oft with difference—yet do they all confirm

    A Turkish fleet, and bearing up to Cyprus.

DUKE OF VENICE

    Nay, it is possible enough to judgment:

    I do not so secure me in the error,

    But the main article I do approve

    In fearful sense.

SAILOR

    [*Within*] What, ho! what, ho! what, ho!

FIRST OFFICER

    A messenger from the galleys.

Enter a Sailor

DUKE OF VENICE

Now, what's the business?

SAILOR

The Turkish preparation makes for Rhodes;
So was I bid report here to the state
By Signior Angelo.

DUKE OF VENICE

How say you by this change?

FIRST SENATOR

This cannot be,
By no assay of reason: 'tis a pageant,
To keep us in false gaze. When we consider
The importancy of Cyprus to the Turk,
And let ourselves again but understand,
That as it more concerns the Turk than Rhodes,
So may he with more facile question bear it,
For that it stands not in such warlike brace,
But altogether lacks the abilities
That Rhodes is dress'd in: if we make thought
      of this,
We must not think the Turk is so unskilful
To leave that latest which concerns him first,
Neglecting an attempt of ease and gain,
To wake and wage a danger profitless.

DUKE OF VENICE

Nay, in all confidence, he's not for Rhodes.

FIRST OFFICER

Here is more news.

Enter a Messenger

MESSENGER

The Ottomites, reverend and gracious,

Steering with due course towards the isle of
Rhodes,

Have there injointed them with an after fleet.

FIRST SENATOR

Ay, so I thought. How many, as you guess?

MESSENGER

Of thirty sail: and now they do restem

Their backward course, bearing with frank
appearance

Their purposes toward Cyprus. Signior
Montano,

Your trusty and most valiant servitor,

With his free duty recommends you thus,

And prays you to believe him.

DUKE OF VENICE

'Tis certain, then, for Cyprus.

Marcus Luccicos, is not he in town?

FIRST SENATOR

He's now in Florence.

DUKE OF VENICE

Write from us to him; post-post-haste dispatch.

FIRST SENATOR

    Here comes Brabantio and the valiant Moor.

    Enter BRABANTIO, OTHELLO,
    IAGO, RODERIGO, and Officers

DUKE OF VENICE

    Valiant Othello, we must straight employ you

    Against the general enemy Ottoman.

    To BRABANTIO

    I did not see you; welcome, gentle signior;

    We lack'd your counsel and your help tonight.

BRABANTIO

    So did I yours. Good your grace, pardon me;

    Neither my place nor aught I heard of business

    Hath raised me from my bed, nor doth the
        general care

    Take hold on me, for my particular grief

    Is of so flood-gate and o'erbearing nature

    That it engluts and swallows other sorrows

    And it is still itself.

DUKE OF VENICE

    Why, what's the matter?

BRABANTIO

    My daughter! O, my daughter!

DUKE OF VENICE AND SENATOR

    Dead?

BRABANTIO

    Ay, to me;

She is abused, stol'n from me, and corrupted
By spells and medicines bought of
   mountebanks;
For nature so preposterously to err,
Being not deficient, blind, or lame of sense,
Sans witchcraft could not.

DUKE OF VENICE

Whoe'er he be that in this foul proceeding
Hath thus beguiled your daughter of herself
And you of her, the bloody book of law
You shall yourself read in the bitter letter
After your own sense, yea, though our
   proper son
Stood in your action.

BRABANTIO

Humbly I thank your grace.
Here is the man, this Moor, whom now, it
   seems,
Your special mandate for the state-affairs
Hath hither brought.

DUKE OF VENICE AND SENATOR

We are very sorry for't.

DUKE OF VENICE

[*To OTHELLO*] What, in your own part, can
you say to this?

BRABANTIO

Nothing, but this is so.

OTHELLO

> Most potent, grave, and reverend signiors,
> My very noble and approved good masters,
> That I have ta'en away this old man's daughter,
> It is most true; true, I have married her:
> The very head and front of my offending
> Hath this extent, no more. Rude am I in my
>   speech,
> And little bless'd with the soft phrase of peace:
> For since these arms of mine had seven years'
>   pith,
> Till now some nine moons wasted, they have
>   used
> Their dearest action in the tented field,
> And little of this great world can I speak,
> More than pertains to feats of broil and battle,
> And therefore little shall I grace my cause
> In speaking for myself. Yet, by your gracious
>   patience,
> I will a round unvarnish'd tale deliver
> Of my whole course of love; what drugs, what
>   charms,
> What conjuration and what mighty magic,
> For such proceeding I am charged withal,
> I won his daughter.

BRABANTIO

> A maiden never bold;

Of spirit so still and quiet, that her motion
Blush'd at herself; and she, in spite of nature,
Of years, of country, credit, every thing,
To fall in love with what she fear'd to look on!
It is a judgment maim'd and most imperfect
That will confess perfection so could err
Against all rules of nature, and must be driven
To find out practises of cunning hell,
Why this should be. I therefore vouch again
That with some mixtures powerful o'er the
    blood,
Or with some dram conjured to this effect,
He wrought upon her.

DUKE OF VENICE

To vouch this, is no proof,
Without more wider and more overt test
Than these thin habits and poor likelihoods
Of modern seeming do prefer against him.

FIRST SENATOR

But, Othello, speak:
Did you by indirect and forced courses
Subdue and poison this young maid's affections?
Or came it by request and such fair question
As soul to soul affordeth?

OTHELLO

I do beseech you,
Send for the lady to the Sagittary,

And let her speak of me before her father:
If you do find me foul in her report,
The trust, the office I do hold of you,
Not only take away, but let your sentence
Even fall upon my life.

DUKE OF VENICE

Fetch Desdemona hither.

OTHELLO

Ancient, conduct them: you best know the
place.

Exeunt IAGO and Attendants

And, till she come, as truly as to heaven
I do confess the vices of my blood,
So justly to your grave ears I'll present
How I did thrive in this fair lady's love,
And she in mine.

DUKE OF VENICE

Say it, Othello.

OTHELLO

Her father loved me; oft invited me;
Still question'd me the story of my life,
From year to year, the battles, sieges, fortunes,
That I have passed.
I ran it through, even from my boyish days,
To the very moment that he bade me tell it;
Wherein I spake of most disastrous chances,
Of moving accidents by flood and field

Of hair-breadth scapes i' the imminent deadly
    breach,
Of being taken by the insolent foe
And sold to slavery, of my redemption thence
And portance in my travels' history:
Wherein of antres vast and deserts idle,
Rough quarries, rocks and hills whose heads
    touch heaven
It was my hint to speak—such was the process;
And of the Cannibals that each other eat,
The Anthropophagi and men whose heads
Do grow beneath their shoulders. This to hear
Would Desdemona seriously incline:
But still the house-affairs would draw her
    thence:
Which ever as she could with haste dispatch,
She'd come again, and with a greedy ear
Devour up my discourse: which I observing,
Took once a pliant hour, and found good means
To draw from her a prayer of earnest heart
That I would all my pilgrimage dilate,
Whereof by parcels she had something heard,
But not intentively: I did consent,
And often did beguile her of her tears,
When I did speak of some distressful stroke
That my youth suffer'd. My story being done,
She gave me for my pains a world of sighs:

She swore, in faith, 'twas strange, 'twas passing
    strange,
'Twas pitiful, 'twas wondrous pitiful:
She wish'd she had not heard it, yet she wish'd
That heaven had made her such a man: she
    thank'd me,
And bade me, if I had a friend that loved her,
I should but teach him how to tell my story.
And that would woo her. Upon this hint I spake:
She loved me for the dangers I had pass'd,
And I loved her that she did pity them.
This only is the witchcraft I have used:
Here comes the lady; let her witness it.
  Enter DESDEMONA, IAGO, and Attendants

DUKE OF VENICE

I think this tale would win my daughter too.
Good Brabantio,
Take up this mangled matter at the best:
Men do their broken weapons rather use
Than their bare hands.

BRABANTIO

I pray you, hear her speak:
If she confess that she was half the wooer,
Destruction on my head, if my bad blame
Light on the man! Come hither, gentle mistress:
Do you perceive in all this noble company
Where most you owe obedience?

DESDEMONA

My noble father,
I do perceive here a divided duty:
To you I am bound for life and education;
My life and education both do learn me
How to respect you; you are the lord of duty;
I am hitherto your daughter: but here's my
    husband,
And so much duty as my mother show'd
To you, preferring you before her father,
So much I challenge that I may profess
Due to the Moor my lord.

BRABANTIO

God be wi' you! I have done.
Please it your grace, on to the state-affairs:
I had rather to adopt a child than get it.
Come hither, Moor:
I here do give thee that with all my heart
Which, but thou hast already, with all my heart
I would keep from thee. For your sake, jewel,
I am glad at soul I have no other child:
For thy escape would teach me tyranny,
To hang clogs on them. I have done, my lord.

DUKE OF VENICE

Let me speak like yourself, and lay a sentence,
Which, as a grise or step, may help these lovers
Into your favour.

When remedies are past, the griefs are ended
By seeing the worst, which late on hopes
    depended.
To mourn a mischief that is past and gone
Is the next way to draw new mischief on.
What cannot be preserved when fortune takes
Patience her injury a mockery makes.
The robb'd that smiles steals something from
    the thief;
He robs himself that spends a bootless grief.

BRABANTIO

So let the Turk of Cyprus us beguile;
We lose it not, so long as we can smile.
He bears the sentence well that nothing bears
But the free comfort which from thence he
    hears,
But he bears both the sentence and the sorrow
That, to pay grief, must of poor patience borrow.
These sentences, to sugar, or to gall,
Being strong on both sides, are equivocal:
But words are words; I never yet did hear
That the bruised heart was pierced through
    the ear.
I humbly beseech you, proceed to the affairs
    of state.

DUKE OF VENICE

The Turk with a most mighty preparation

makes for Cyprus. Othello, the fortitude of the place is best known to you; and though we have there a substitute of most allowed sufficiency, yet opinion, a sovereign mistress of effects, throws a more safer voice on you: you must therefore be content to slubber the gloss of your new fortunes with this more stubborn and boisterous expedition.

OTHELLO

The tyrant custom, most grave senators,
Hath made the flinty and steel couch of war
My thrice-driven bed of down: I do agnise
A natural and prompt alacrity
I find in hardness, and do undertake
These present wars against the Ottomites.
Most humbly therefore bending to your state,
I crave fit disposition for my wife.
Due reference of place and exhibition,
With such accommodation and besort
As levels with her breeding.

DUKE OF VENICE

If you please,
Be't at her father's.

BRABANTIO

I'll not have it so.

OTHELLO

Nor I.

DESDEMONA

> Nor I; I would not there reside,
> To put my father in impatient thoughts
> By being in his eye. Most gracious Duke,
> To my unfolding lend your prosperous ear;
> And let me find a charter in your voice,
> To assist my simpleness.

DUKE OF VENICE

> What would you, Desdemona?

DESDEMONA

> That I did love the Moor to live with him,
> My downright violence and storm of fortunes
> May trumpet to the world: my heart's subdued
> Even to the very quality of my lord:
> I saw Othello's visage in his mind,
> And to his honour and his valiant parts
> Did I my soul and fortunes consecrate.
> So that, dear lords, if I be left behind,
> A moth of peace, and he go to the war,
> The rites for which I love him are bereft me,
> And I a heavy interim shall support
> By his dear absence. Let me go with him.

OTHELLO

> Let her have your voices.
> Vouch with me, heaven, I therefore beg it not,
> To please the palate of my appetite,
> Nor to comply with heat—the young affects

In me defunct—and proper satisfaction.
But to be free and bounteous to her mind:
And heaven defend your good souls, that you
 think
I will your serious and great business scant
For she is with me: no, when light-wing'd toys
Of feather'd Cupid seal with wanton dullness
My speculative and officed instruments,
That my disports corrupt and taint my business,
Let housewives make a skillet of my helm,
And all indign and base adversities
Make head against my estimation!

DUKE OF VENICE

Be it as you shall privately determine,
Either for her stay or going: the affair cries
 haste,
And speed must answer it.

FIRST SENATOR

You must away to-night.

DESDEMONA

To-night, my lord!

DUKE OF VENICE

This night.

OTHELLO

With all my heart.

DUKE OF VENICE

At nine i' the morning here we'll meet again.

Othello, leave some officer behind,
And he shall our commission bring to you;
With such things else of quality and respect
As doth import you.

OTHELLO

So please your grace, my ancient;
A man he is of honest and trust:
To his conveyance I assign my wife,
With what else needful your good grace
    shall think
To be sent after me.

DUKE OF VENICE

Let it be so.
Good night to every one.

> *To BRABANTIO*

And, noble signior,
If virtue no delighted beauty lack,
Your son-in-law is far more fair than black.

FIRST SENATOR

Adieu, brave Moor, use Desdemona well.

BRABANTIO

Look to her, Moor, if thou hast eyes to see:
She has deceived her father, and may thee.

> *Exeunt DUKE OF VENICE,*
> *Senators, Officers, & c.*

OTHELLO

My life upon her faith! Honest Iago,

My Desdemona must I leave to thee:
I prithee, let thy wife attend on her:
And bring them after in the best advantage.
Come, Desdemona: I have but an hour
Of love, of worldly matters and direction,
To spend with thee: we must obey the time.

Exeunt OTHELLO and DESDEMONA

RODERIGO

Iago—

IAGO

What say'st thou, noble heart?

RODERIGO

What will I do, thinkest thou?

IAGO

Why, go to bed, and sleep.

RODERIGO

I will incontinently drown myself.

IAGO

If thou dost, I shall never love thee after. Why,
thou silly gentleman!

RODERIGO

It is silliness to live when to live is torment;
and then have we a prescription to die when
death is our physician.

IAGO

O villainous! I have looked upon the world
for four times seven years; and since I could

distinguish betwixt a benefit and an injury, I never found man that knew how to love himself. Ere I would say, I would drown myself for the love of a guinea-hen, I would change my humanity with a baboon.

RODERIGO

What should I do? I confess it is my shame to be so fond; but it is not in my virtue to amend it.

IAGO

Virtue! a fig! 'tis in ourselves that we are thus or thus. Our bodies are our gardens, to the which our wills are gardeners: so that if we will plant nettles, or sow lettuce, set hyssop and weed up thyme, supply it with one gender of herbs, or distract it with many, either to have it sterile with idleness, or manured with industry, why, the power and corrigible authority of this lies in our wills. If the balance of our lives had not one scale of reason to poise another of sensuality, the blood and baseness of our natures would conduct us to most preposterous conclusions: but we have reason to cool our raging motions, our carnal stings, our unbitted lusts, whereof I take this that you call love to be a sect or scion.

RODERIGO

It cannot be.

IAGO

It is merely a lust of the blood and a permission of the will. Come, be a man. Drown thyself! drown cats and blind puppies. I have professed me thy friend and I confess me knit to thy deserving with cables of perdurable toughness; I could never better stead thee than now. Put money in thy purse; follow thou the wars; defeat thy favour with an usurped beard; I say, put money in thy purse. It cannot be that Desdemona should long continue her love to the Moor—put money in thy purse—nor he his to her: it was a violent commencement, and thou shalt see an answerable sequestration:— put but money in thy purse. These Moors are changeable in their wills: fill thy purse with money:—the food that to him now is as luscious as locusts, shall be to him shortly as bitter as coloquintida. She must change for youth: when she is sated with his body, she will find the error of her choice: she must have change, she must: therefore put money in thy purse. If thou wilt needs damn thyself, do it a more delicate way than drowning. Make all the money thou canst: if sanctimony and a frail vow betwixt an erring barbarian and a super-subtle Venetian not too hard for my

wits and all the tribe of hell, thou shalt enjoy
her; therefore make money. A pox of drowning
thyself! it is clean out of the way: seek thou
rather to be hanged in compassing thy joy than
to be drowned and go without her.

RODERIGO

Wilt thou be fast to my hopes, if I depend on
the issue?

IAGO

Thou art sure of me:—go, make money:—I
have told thee often, and I re-tell thee again
and again, I hate the Moor: my cause is
hearted; thine hath no less reason. Let us be
conjunctive in our revenge against him: if thou
canst cuckold him, thou dost thyself a pleasure,
me a sport. There are many events in the womb
of time which will be delivered. Traverse! go,
provide thy money. We will have more of this
to-morrow. Adieu.

RODERIGO

Where shall we meet i' the morning?

IAGO

At my lodging.

RODERIGO

I'll be with thee betimes.

IAGO

Go to; farewell. Do you hear, Roderigo?

RODERIGO

What say you?

IAGO

No more of drowning, do you hear?

RODERIGO

I am changed.

IAGO

Go to; farewell. Put money enough in your purse.

RODERIGO

I'll go sell all my land.

Exit RODERIGO

IAGO

Thus do I ever make my fool my purse:
For I mine own gain'd knowledge should profane,
If I would time expend with such a snipe.
But for my sport and profit. I hate the Moor:
And it is thought abroad, that 'twixt my sheets
He has done my office: I know not if't be true;
But I, for mere suspicion in that kind,
Will do as if for surety. He holds me well;
The better shall my purpose work on him.
Cassio's a proper man: let me see now:
To get his place and to plume up my will
In double knavery—How, how? Let's see:—
After some time, to abuse Othello's ear

That he is too familiar with his wife.
He hath a person and a smooth dispose
To be suspected, framed to make women false.
The Moor is of a free and open nature,
That thinks men honest that but seem to be so,
And will as tenderly be led by the nose
As asses are.
I have't. It is engender'd. Hell and night
Must bring this monstrous birth to the world's
    light.

Exit

Act II

SCENE I. A SEA-PORT IN CYPRUS. AN OPEN PLACE NEAR THE QUAY.

Enter MONTANO and two Gentlemen

MONTANO

What from the cape can you discern at sea?

FIRST GENTLEMAN

Nothing at all: it is a high-wrought flood;

I cannot, 'twixt the heaven and the main,

Descry a sail.

MONTANO

Methinks the wind hath spoke aloud at land;

A fuller blast ne'er shook our battlements:

If it hath ruffian'd so upon the sea,

What ribs of oak, when mountains melt on them,

Can hold the mortise? What shall we hear of this?

SECOND GENTLEMAN

A segregation of the Turkish fleet:
For do but stand upon the foaming shore,
The chidden billow seems to pelt the clouds;
The wind-shaked surge, with high and monstrous mane,
Seems to cast water on the burning bear,
And quench the guards of the ever-fixed pole:
I never did like molestation view
On the enchafed flood.

MONTANO

If that the Turkish fleet
Be not enshelter'd and embay'd, they are drown'd:
It is impossible they bear it out.

Enter a third Gentleman

THIRD GENTLEMAN

News, lads! our wars are done.
The desperate tempest hath so bang'd the Turks,
That their designment halts: a noble ship of Venice
Hath seen a grievous wreck and sufferance
On most part of their fleet.

MONTANO

How! Is this true?

THIRD GENTLEMAN

    The ship is here put in,

    A Veronesa; Michael Cassio,

    Lieutenant to the warlike Moor Othello,

    Is come on shore: the Moor himself at sea,

    And is in full commission here for Cyprus.

MONTANO

    I am glad on't; 'tis a worthy governor.

THIRD GENTLEMAN

    But this same Cassio, though he speak of comfort

    Touching the Turkish loss, yet he looks sadly,

    And prays the Moor be safe; for they were parted

    With foul and violent tempest.

MONTANO

    Pray heavens he be;

    For I have served him, and the man commands

    Like a full soldier. Let's to the seaside, ho!

    As well to see the vessel that's come in

    As to throw out our eyes for brave Othello,

    Even till we make the main and the aerial blue

    An indistinct regard.

THIRD GENTLEMAN

    Come, let's do so:

    For every minute is expectancy

    Of more arrivance.

Enter CASSIO

CASSIO

Thanks, you the valiant of this warlike isle,
That so approve the Moor! O, let the heavens
Give him defence against the elements,
For I have lost us him on a dangerous sea.

MONTANO

Is he well shipp'd?

CASSIO

His bark is stoutly timber'd, his pilot
Of very expert and approved allowance;
Therefore my hopes, not surfeited to death,
Stand in bold cure.

A cry within 'A sail, a sail, a sail!'
Enter a Messenger

CASSIO

What noise?

MESSENGER

The town is empty; on the brow o' the sea
Stand ranks of people, and they cry 'A sail!'

CASSIO

My hopes do shape him for the governor.
Guns heard

SECOND GENTLEMAN

They do discharge their shot of courtesy:
Our friends at least.

CASSIO

    I pray you, sir, go forth,

    And give us truth who 'tis that is arrived.

SECOND GENTLEMAN

    I shall.

Exit

MONTANO

    But, good lieutenant, is your general wived?

CASSIO

    Most fortunately: he hath achieved a maid

    That paragons description and wild fame;

    One that excels the quirks of blazoning pens,

    And in the essential vesture of creation

    Does tire the ingener.

Re-enter second Gentleman

    How now! Who has put in?

SECOND GENTLEMAN

    'Tis one Iago, ancient to the general.

CASSIO

    'Has had most favourable and happy speed:

    Tempests themselves, high seas, and howling
        winds,

    The gutter'd rocks and congregated sands—

    Traitors ensteep'd to clog the guiltless keel,

    As having sense of beauty, do omit

    Their mortal natures, letting go safely by

    The divine Desdemona.

MONTANO

What is she?

CASSIO

She that I spake of, our great captain's captain,
Left in the conduct of the bold Iago,
Whose footing here anticipates our thoughts
A se'nnight's speed. Great Jove, Othello guard,
And swell his sail with thine own powerful
    breath,
That he may bless this bay with his tall ship,
Make love's quick pants in Desdemona's arms,
Give renew'd fire to our extinted spirits
And bring all Cyprus comfort!

    Enter DESDEMONA, EMILIA,
    IAGO, RODERIGO, and Attendants

O, behold,
The riches of the ship is come on shore!
Ye men of Cyprus, let her have your knees.
Hail to thee, lady! and the grace of heaven,
Before, behind thee, and on every hand,
Enwheel thee round!

DESDEMONA

I thank you, valiant Cassio.
What tidings can you tell me of my lord?

CASSIO

He is not yet arrived: nor know I aught
But that he's well and will be shortly here.

DESDEMONA

O, but I fear—How lost you company?

CASSIO

The great contention of the sea and skies
Parted our fellowship—But, hark! a sail.

Within: 'A sail, a sail!' Guns heard

SECOND GENTLEMAN

They give their greeting to the citadel;
This likewise is a friend.

CASSIO

See for the news.

Exit Gentleman

Good ancient, you are welcome.

To EMILIA

Welcome, mistress.
Let it not gall your patience, good Iago,
That I extend my manners; 'tis my breeding
That gives me this bold show of courtesy.

Kissing her

IAGO

Sir, would she give you so much of her lips
As of her tongue she oft bestows on me,
You'll have enough.

DESDEMONA

Alas, she has no speech.

IAGO

In faith, too much;

I find it still, when I have list to sleep:
Marry, before your ladyship, I grant,
She puts her tongue a little in her heart,
And chides with thinking.

EMILIA

You have little cause to say so.

IAGO

Come on, come on; you are pictures out of doors, Bells in your parlors, wild-cats in your kitchens, Saints m your injuries, devils being offended, Players in your housewifery, and housewives' in your beds.

DESDEMONA

O, fie upon thee, slanderer!

IAGO

Nay, it is true, or else I am a Turk:
You rise to play and go to bed to work.

EMILIA

You shall not write my praise.

IAGO

No, let me not.

DESDEMONA

What wouldst thou write of me, if thou shouldst praise me?

IAGO

O gentle lady, do not put me to't;
For I am nothing, if not critical.

DESDEMONA

Come on assay. There's one gone to the
harbour?

IAGO

Ay, madam.

DESDEMONA

I am not merry; but I do beguile
The thing I am, by seeming otherwise.
Come, how wouldst thou praise me?

IAGO

I am about it; but indeed my invention
Comes from my pate as birdlime does from
frize;
It plucks out brains and all: but my Muse
labours,
And thus she is deliver'd.
If she be fair and wise, fairness and wit,
The one's for use, the other useth it.

DESDEMONA

Well praised! How if she be black and witty?

IAGO

If she be black, and thereto have a wit,
She'll find a white that shall her blackness fit.

DESDEMONA

Worse and worse.

EMILIA

How if fair and foolish?

IAGO

She never yet was foolish that was fair;

For even her folly help'd her to an heir.

DESDEMONA

These are old fond paradoxes to make fools laugh i' the alehouse. What miserable praise hast thou for her that's foul and foolish?

IAGO

There's none so foul and foolish thereunto,

But does foul pranks which fair and wise ones do.

DESDEMONA

O heavy ignorance! thou praisest the worst best. But what praise couldst thou bestow on a deserving woman indeed, one that, in the authority of her merit, did justly put on the vouch of very malice itself?

IAGO

She that was ever fair and never proud,

Had tongue at will and yet was never loud,

Never lack'd gold and yet went never gay,

Fled from her wish and yet said 'Now I may,'

She that being anger'd, her revenge being nigh,

Bade her wrong stay and her displeasure fly,

She that in wisdom never was so frail

To change the cod's head for the salmon's tail;

She that could think and ne'er disclose her mind,

See suitors following and not look behind,
She was a wight, if ever such wight were—

DESDEMONA

To do what?

IAGO

To suckle fools and chronicle small beer.

DESDEMONA

O most lame and impotent conclusion! Do not learn of him, Emilia, though he be thy husband. How say you, Cassio? is he not a most profane and liberal counsellor?

CASSIO

He speaks home, madam: You may relish him more in the soldier than in the scholar.

IAGO

[*Aside*] He takes her by the palm: ay, well said, whisper: with as little a web as this will I ensnare as great a fly as Cassio. Ay, smile upon her, do; I will gyve thee in thine own courtship. You say true; 'tis so, indeed: if such tricks as these strip you out of your lieutenantry, it had been better you had not kissed your three fingers so oft, which now again you are most apt to play the sir in. Very good; well kissed! an excellent courtesy! 'tis so, indeed. Yet again your fingers to your lips? would they were clyster-pipes for your sake!

Trumpet within

The Moor! I know his trumpet.

CASSIO

'Tis truly so.

DESDEMONA

Let's meet him and receive him.

CASSIO

Lo, where he comes!

Enter OTHELLO and Attendants

OTHELLO

O my fair warrior!

DESDEMONA

My dear Othello!

OTHELLO

It gives me wonder great as my content

To see you here before me. O my soul's joy!

If after every tempest come such calms,

May the winds blow till they have waken'd
    death!

And let the labouring bark climb hills of seas

Olympus-high and duck again as low

As hell's from heaven! If it were now to die,

'Twere now to be most happy; for, I fear,

My soul hath her content so absolute

That not another comfort like to this

Succeeds in unknown fate.

DESDEMONA

    The heavens forbid

    But that our loves and comforts should increase,

    Even as our days do grow!

OTHELLO

    Amen to that, sweet powers!

    I cannot speak enough of this content;

    It stops me here; it is too much of joy:

    And this, and this, the greatest discords be

               Kissing her

    That e'er our hearts shall make!

IAGO

    [*Aside*] O, you are well tuned now!

    But I'll set down the pegs that make this music,

    As honest as I am.

OTHELLO

    Come, let us to the castle.

    News, friends; our wars are done, the Turks are
        drown'd.

    How does my old acquaintance of this isle?

    Honey, you shall be well desired in Cyprus;

    I have found great love amongst them. O my
        sweet,

    I prattle out of fashion, and I dote

    In mine own comforts. I prithee, good Iago,

    Go to the bay and disembark my coffers:

    Bring thou the master to the citadel;

He is a good one, and his worthiness
Does challenge much respect. Come, Desdemona,
Once more, well met at Cyprus.

> *Exeunt OTHELLO,*
> *DESDEMONA, and Attendants*

IAGO

[*To one leaving*] Do thou meet me presently at the harbour. [*To RODERIGO*] Come hither. If thou be'st valiant—as, they say, base men being in love have then a nobility in their natures more than is native to them—list me. The lieutenant tonight watches on the court of guard:—first, I must tell thee this— Desdemona is directly in love with him.

RODERIGO

With him! Why, 'tis not possible.

IAGO

Lay thy finger thus, and let thy soul be instructed. Mark me with what violence she first loved the Moor, but for bragging and telling her fantastical lies: and will she love him still for prating? Let not thy discreet heart think it. Her eye must be fed; and what delight shall she have to look on the devil? When the blood is made dull with the act of sport, there should be, again to inflame it and to give satiety a fresh appetite, loveliness in favour, sympathy in years, manners and beauties; all which the Moor is defective in: now, for want of these required conveniences, her delicate tenderness will find itself abused, begin to heave the gorge, disrelish and abhor the Moor; very nature will instruct her in it and compel her to some second choice. Now, sir, this granted—as it is a most pregnant and unforced position—who stands so eminent in the degree of this fortune as Cassio does? A knave very voluble; no further conscionable than in putting on the mere form of civil and humane seeming, for the better compassing of his salt and most hidden loose affection? Why, none; why, none: a slipper and subtle knave, a finder of occasions, that has an eye can stamp and counterfeit advantages, though true advantage never present itself; a devilish knave. Besides, the knave is handsome, young, and hath all those requisites in him that folly and green minds look after: a pestilent complete knave; and the woman hath found him already.

RODERIGO

I cannot believe that in her; she's full of most blessed condition.

IAGO

Blessed fig's-end! the wine she drinks is made of grapes: if she had been blessed, she would never have loved the Moor. Blessed pudding! Didst thou not see her paddle with the palm of his hand? Didst not mark that?

RODERIGO

Yes, that I did; but that was but courtesy.

IAGO

Lechery, by this hand; an index and obscure prologue to the history of lust and foul thoughts. They met so near with their lips that their breaths embraced together. Villainous thoughts, Roderigo! when these mutualities so marshal the way, hard at hand comes the master and main exercise, the incorporate conclusion, Pish! But, sir, be you ruled by me: I have brought you from Venice. Watch you to-night; for the command, I'll lay't upon you. Cassio knows you not. I'll not be far from you: do you find some occasion to anger Cassio, either by speaking too loud, or tainting his discipline; or from what other course you please, which the time shall more favourably minister.

RODERIGO

Well.

IAGO

> Sir, he is rash and very sudden in choler, and
> haply with his truncheon may strike at you:
> provoke him, that he may; for even out of that
> will I cause these of Cyprus to mutiny; whose
> qualification shall come into no true taste
> again but by the displanting of Cassio. So shall
> you have a shorter journey to your desires by
> the means I shall then have to prefer them;
> and the impediment most profitably removed,
> without the which there were no expectation
> of our prosperity.

RODERIGO

> I will do this, if I can bring it to any opportunity.

IAGO

> I warrant thee. Meet me by and by at the citadel:
> I must fetch his necessaries ashore. Farewell.

RODERIGO

> Adieu.

Exit

IAGO

> That Cassio loves her, I do well believe it;
> That she loves him, 'tis apt and of great credit:
> The Moor, howbeit that I endure him not,
> Is of a constant, loving, noble nature,
> And I dare think he'll prove to Desdemona
> A most dear husband. Now, I do love her too;

Not out of absolute lust, though per-adventure
I stand accountant for as great a sin,
But partly led to diet my revenge,
For that I do suspect the lusty Moor
Hath leap'd into my seat; the thought whereof
Doth, like a poisonous mineral, gnaw my
    inwards;
And nothing can or shall content my soul
Till I am even'd with him, wife for wife,
Or failing so, yet that I put the Moor
At least into a jealousy so strong
That judgment cannot cure. Which thing to do,
If this poor trash of Venice, whom I trash
For his quick hunting, stand the putting on,
I'll have our Michael Cassio on the hip,
Abuse him to the Moor in the rank garb—
For I fear Cassio with my night-cap too—
Make the Moor thank me, love me and
    reward me.
For making him egregiously an ass
And practising upon his peace and quiet
Even to madness. 'Tis here, but yet confused:
Knavery's plain face is never seen tin used.

Exit

SCENE II. A STREET.

Enter a Herald with a proclamation; People following
HERALD

It is Othello's pleasure, our noble and valiant
general, that, upon certain tidings now arrived,
importing the mere perdition of the Turkish
fleet, every man put himself into triumph;
some to dance, some to make bonfires, each
man to what sport and revels his addiction
leads him: for, besides these beneficial news, it
is the celebration of his nuptial. So much was
his pleasure should be proclaimed. All offices
are open, and there is full liberty of feasting
from this present hour of five till the bell have
told eleven. Heaven bless the isle of Cyprus
and our noble general Othello!

Exeunt

SCENE III. A HALL IN THE CASTLE.

*Enter OTHELLO, DESDEMONA, CASSIO, and
Attendants*
OTHELLO

Good Michael, look you to the guard to-night:
Let's teach ourselves that honourable stop,
Not to outsport discretion.

CASSIO

Iago hath direction what to do;

But, notwithstanding, with my personal eye

Will I look to't.

OTHELLO

Iago is most honest.

Michael, good night: to-morrow with your earliest

Let me have speech with you.

To DESDEMONA

Come, my dear love,

The purchase made, the fruits are to ensue;

That profit's yet to come 'tween me and you.

Good night.

Exeunt OTHELLO,
DESDEMONA, and Attendants
Enter IAGO

CASSIO

Welcome, Iago; we must to the watch.

IAGO

Not this hour, lieutenant; 'tis not yet ten o' the clock. Our general cast us thus early for the love of his Desdemona; who let us not therefore blame: he hath not yet made wanton the night with her; and she is sport for Jove.

CASSIO

She's a most exquisite lady.

IAGO

And, I'll warrant her, fun of game.

CASSIO

Indeed, she's a most fresh and delicate creature.

IAGO

What an eye she has! methinks it sounds a parley of provocation.

CASSIO

An inviting eye; and yet methinks right modest.

IAGO

And when she speaks, is it not an alarm to love?

CASSIO

She is indeed perfection.

IAGO

Well, happiness to their sheets! Come, lieutenant, I have a stoup of wine; and here without are a brace of Cyprus gallants that would fain have a measure to the health of black Othello.

CASSIO

Not to-night, good Iago: I have very poor and unhappy brains for drinking: I could well wish courtesy would invent some other custom of entertainment.

IAGO

O, they are our friends; but one cup: I'll drink for you.

CASSIO

I have drunk but one cup to-night, and that
was craftily qualified too, and, behold, what
innovation it makes here: I am unfortunate in
the infirmity, and dare not task my weakness
with any more.

IAGO

What, man! 'tis a night of revels: the gallants
desire it.

CASSIO

Where are they?

IAGO

Here at the door; I pray you, call them in.

CASSIO

I'll do't; but it dislikes me.

Exit

IAGO

If I can fasten but one cup upon him,
With that which he hath drunk to-night already,
He'll be as full of quarrel and offence
As my young mistress' dog. Now, my sick fool
    Roderigo,
Whom love hath turn'd almost the wrong
    side out,
To Desdemona hath to-night caroused
Potations pottle deep; and he's to watch:
Three lads of Cyprus, noble swelling spirits,

That hold their honours in a wary distance,
The very elements of this warlike isle,
Have I to-night fluster'd with flowing cups,
And they watch too. Now, 'mongst this flock
     of drunkards,
Am I to put our Cassio in some action
That may offend the isle—but here they come:
If consequence do but approve my dream,
My boat sails freely, both with wind and stream.
Re-enter CASSIO; with him MONTANO and
     Gentlemen; servants following with wine

CASSIO
     'Fore God, they have given me a rouse already.
MONTANO
     Good faith, a little one; not past a pint, as I am
     a soldier.
IAGO
     Some wine, ho!
     Sings
     And let me the canakin clink, clink;
     And let me the canakin clink
     A soldier's a man;
     A life's but a span;
     Why, then, let a soldier drink.
     Some wine, boys!
CASSIO
     'Fore God, an excellent song.

IAGO

I learned it in England, where, indeed, they
are most potent in potting: your Dane, your
German, and your swag-bellied Hollander—
Drink, ho!—are nothing to your English.

CASSIO

Is your Englishman so expert in his drinking?

IAGO

Why, he drinks you, with facility, your Dane
dead drunk; he sweats not to overthrow your
Almain; he gives your Hollander a vomit, ere
the next pottle can be filled.

CASSIO

To the health of our general!

MONTANO

I am for it, lieutenant; and I'll do you justice.

IAGO

O sweet England!

Sings

King Stephen was a worthy peer,
His breeches cost him but a crown;
He held them sixpence all too dear,
With that he call'd the tailor lown.
He was a wight of high renown,
And thou art but of low degree:
'Tis pride that pulls the country down;

Then take thine auld cloak about thee.
Some wine, ho!

CASSIO

Why, this is a more exquisite song than the
other.

IAGO

Will you hear't again?

CASSIO

No; for I hold him to be unworthy of his place
that does those things. Well, God's above all;
and there be souls must be saved, and there be
souls must not be saved.

IAGO

It's true, good lieutenant.

CASSIO

For mine own part—no offence to the general,
nor any man of quality—I hope to be saved.

IAGO

And so do I too, lieutenant.

CASSIO

Ay, but, by your leave, not before me; the
lieutenant is to be saved before the ancient.
Let's have no more of this; let's to our affairs.
Forgive us our sins! Gentlemen, let's look to
our business. Do not think, gentlemen. I am
drunk: this is my ancient; this is my right hand,

and this is my left: I am not drunk now; I can
stand well enough, and speak well enough.

ALL

Excellent well.

CASSIO

Why, very well then; you must not think then
that I am drunk.

Exit

MONTANO

To the platform, masters; come, let's set the
watch.

IAGO

You see this fellow that is gone before;
He is a soldier fit to stand by Caesar
And give direction: and do but see his vice;
'Tis to his virtue a just equinox,
The one as long as the other: 'tis pity of him.
I fear the trust Othello puts him in.
On some odd time of his infirmity,
Will shake this island.

MONTANO

But is he often thus?

IAGO

'Tis evermore the prologue to his sleep:
He'll watch the horologe a double set,
If drink rock not his cradle.

MONTANO

    It were well

    The general were put in mind of it.

    Perhaps he sees it not; or his good nature

    Prizes the virtue that appears in Cassio,

    And looks not on his evils: is not this true?

              Enter RODERIGO

IAGO

    [*Aside to him*] How now, Roderigo!

    I pray you, after the lieutenant; go.

                   Exit RODERIGO

MONTANO

    And 'tis great pity that the noble Moor

    Should hazard such a place as his own second

    With one of an ingraft infirmity:

    It were an honest action to say

    So to the Moor.

IAGO

    Not I, for this fair island:

    I do love Cassio well; and would do much

    To cure him of this evil—But, hark! What
        noise?

          Cry within: 'Help! help!'

    Re-enter CASSIO, driving in RODERIGO

CASSIO

    You rogue! You rascal!

MONTANO

What's the matter, lieutenant?

CASSIO

A knave teach me my duty! I'll beat the knave
into a twiggen bottle.

RODERIGO

Beat me!

CASSIO

Dost thou prate, rogue?

Striking RODERIGO

MONTANO

Nay, good lieutenant;

Staying him

I pray you, sir, hold your hand.

CASSIO

Let me go, sir,
Or I'll knock you o'er the mazzard.

MONTANO

Come, come, you're drunk.

CASSIO

Drunk!

They fight

IAGO

[*Aside to RODERIGO*] Away, I say; go out, and
cry a mutiny.

Exit RODERIGO

Nay, good lieutenant—alas, gentlemen—

Help, ho!—Lieutenant—sir—Montano—sir;
Help, masters!—Here's a goodly watch indeed!

Bell rings

Who's that which rings the bell? Diablo, ho!
The town will rise: God's will, lieutenant, hold!
You will be shamed for ever.

Re-enter OTHELLO and Attendants

OTHELLO

What is the matter here?

MONTANO

Zounds, I bleed still; I am hurt to the death.

Faints

OTHELLO

Hold, for your lives!

IAGO

Hold, ho! Lieutenant—sir—Montano—
gentlemen—
Have you forgot all sense of place and duty?
Hold! the general speaks to you; hold, hold, for
shame!

OTHELLO

Why, how now, ho! from whence ariseth this?
Are we turn'd Turks, and to ourselves do that
Which heaven hath forbid the Ottomites?
For Christian shame, put by this barbarous
brawl:
He that stirs next to carve for his own rage

Holds his soul light; he dies upon his motion.
Silence that dreadful bell: it frights the isle
From her propriety. What is the matter, masters?
Honest Iago, that look'st dead with grieving,
Speak, who began this? On thy love, I charge thee.

IAGO

I do not know: friends all but now, even now,
In quarter, and in terms like bride and groom
Divesting them for bed; and then, but now—
As if some planet had unwitted men—
Swords out, and tilting one at other's breast,
In opposition bloody. I cannot speak
Any beginning to this peevish odds;
And would in action glorious I had lost
Those legs that brought me to a part of it!

OTHELLO

How comes it, Michael, you are thus forgot?

CASSIO

I pray you, pardon me; I cannot speak.

OTHELLO

Worthy Montano, you were wont be civil;
The gravity and stillness of your youth
The world hath noted, and your name is great
In mouths of wisest censure: what's the matter,
That you unlace your reputation thus
And spend your rich opinion for the name
Of a night-brawler? Give me answer to it.

MONTANO

    Worthy Othello, I am hurt to danger:

    Your officer, Iago, can inform you,

    While I spare speech, which something now
        offends me,

    Of all that I do know: nor know I aught

    By me that's said or done amiss this night;

    Unless self-charity be sometimes a vice,

    And to defend ourselves it be a sin

    When violence assails us.

OTHELLO

    Now, by heaven,

    My blood begins my safer guides to rule;

    And passion, having my best judgment collied,

    Assays to lead the way: if I once stir,

    Or do but lift this arm, the best of you

    Shall sink in my rebuke. Give me to know

    How this foul rout began, who set it on;

    And he that is approved in this offence,

    Though he had twinn'd with me, both at a birth,

    Shall lose me. What! in a town of war,

    Yet wild, the people's hearts brimful of fear,

    To manage private and domestic quarrel,

    In night, and on the court and guard of safety!

    'Tis monstrous. Iago, who began't?

MONTANO

    If partially affined, or leagued in office,

Thou dost deliver more or less than truth,
Thou art no soldier.

IAGO
Touch me not so near:
I had rather have this tongue cut from my
mouth
Than it should do offence to Michael Cassio;
Yet, I persuade myself, to speak the truth
Shall nothing wrong him. Thus it is, general.
Montano and myself being in speech,
There comes a fellow crying out for help:
And Cassio following him with determined
sword,
To execute upon him. Sir, this gentleman
Steps in to Cassio, and entreats his pause:
Myself the crying fellow did pursue,
Lest by his clamour—as it so fell out—
The town might fall in fright: he, swift of foot,
Outran my purpose; and I return'd the rather
For that I heard the clink and fall of swords,
And Cassio high in oath; which till to-night
I ne'er might say before. When I came back—
For this was brief—I found them close together,
At blow and thrust; even as again they were
When you yourself did part them.
More of this matter cannot I report:
But men are men; the best sometimes forget:

Though Cassio did some little wrong to him,
As men in rage strike those that wish them best,
Yet surely Cassio, I believe, received
From him that fled some strange indignity,
Which patience could not pass.

OTHELLO

I know, Iago,
Thy honesty and love doth mince this matter,
Making it light to Cassio. Cassio, I love thee
But never more be officer of mine.

Re-enter DESDEMONA, attended

Look, if my gentle love be not raised up!
I'll make thee an example.

DESDEMONA

What's the matter?

OTHELLO

All's well now, sweeting; come away to bed.
[*To MONTANIO*]
Sir, for your hurts, myself will be your surgeon:
Lead him off.

MONTANO is led off

Iago, look with care about the town,
And silence those whom this vile brawl
    distracted.
Come, Desdemona: 'tis the soldiers' life
To have their balmy slumbers waked with strife.

Exeunt all but IAGO and CASSIO

IAGO

What, are you hurt, lieutenant?

CASSIO

Ay, past all surgery.

IAGO

Marry, heaven forbid!

CASSIO

Reputation, reputation, reputation! O, I have lost my reputation! I have lost the immortal part of myself, and what remains is bestial. My reputation, Iago, my reputation!

IAGO

As I am an honest man, I thought you had received some bodily wound; there is more sense in that than in reputation. Reputation is an idle and most false imposition: oft got without merit, and lost without deserving: you have lost no reputation at all, unless you repute yourself such a loser. What, man! there are ways to recover the general again: you are but now cast in his mood, a punishment more in policy than in malice, even so as one would beat his offenceless dog to affright an imperious lion: sue to him again, and he's yours.

CASSIO

I will rather sue to be despised than to deceive so good a commander with so slight, so drunken, and so indiscreet an officer. Drunk! And speak parrot! And squabble, swagger, swear! And discourse fustian with one's own shadow! O thou invisible spirit of wine, if thou hast no name to be known by, let us call thee devil!

IAGO

What was he that you followed with your sword? What had he done to you?

CASSIO

I know not.

IAGO

Is't possible?

CASSIO

I remember a mass of things, but nothing distinctly; a quarrel, but nothing wherefore. O God, that men should put an enemy in their mouths to steal away their brains! that we should, with joy, pleasance revel and applause, transform ourselves into beasts!

IAGO

Why, but you are now well enough: how came you thus recovered?

CASSIO

It hath pleased the devil drunkenness to give place to the devil wrath; one unperfectness shows me another, to make me frankly despise myself.

IAGO

Come, you are too severe a moraler: as the time, the place, and the condition of this country stands, I could heartily wish this had not befallen; but, since it is as it is, mend it for your own good.

CASSIO

I will ask him for my place again; he shall tell me I am a drunkard! Had I as many mouths as Hydra, such an answer would stop them all. To be now a sensible man, by and by a fool, and presently a beast! O strange! Every inordinate cup is unblessed and the ingredient is a devil.

IAGO

Come, come, good wine is a good familiar creature, if it be well used: exclaim no more against it. And, good lieutenant, I think you think I love you.

CASSIO

I have well approved it, sir. I drunk!

IAGO

You or any man living may be drunk! at a time, man. I'll tell you what you shall do. Our general's wife is now the general: may say so in this respect, for that he hath devoted and given up himself to the contemplation, mark, and denotement of her parts and graces: confess yourself freely to her; importune her help to put you in your place again: she is of so free, so kind, so apt, so blessed a disposition, she holds it a vice in her goodness not to do more than she is requested: this broken joint between you and her husband entreat her to splinter; and, my fortunes against any lay worth naming, this crack of your love shall grow stronger than it was before.

CASSIO

You advise me well.

IAGO

I protest, in the sincerity of love and honest kindness.

CASSIO

I think it freely; and betimes in the morning I will beseech the virtuous Desdemona to undertake for me: I am desperate of my fortunes if they check me here.

IAGO

You are in the right. Good night, lieutenant; I must to the watch.

CASSIO

Good night, honest Iago.

Exit

IAGO

And what's he then that says I play the villain?

When this advice is free I give and honest,
Probal to thinking and indeed the course
To win the Moor again? For 'tis most easy
The inclining Desdemona to subdue
In any honest suit: she's framed as fruitful
As the free elements. And then for her
To win the Moor—were't to renounce his
    baptism,
All seals and symbols of redeemed sin,
His soul is so enfetter'd to her love,
That she may make, unmake, do what she list,
Even as her appetite shall play the god
With his weak function. How am I then a villain
To counsel Cassio to this parallel course,
Directly to his good? Divinity of hell!
When devils will the blackest sins put on,
They do suggest at first with heavenly shows,
As I do now: for whiles this honest fool
Plies Desdemona to repair his fortunes
And she for him pleads strongly to the Moor,
I'll pour this pestilence into his ear,
That she repeals him for her body's lust;
And by how much she strives to do him good,
She shall undo her credit with the Moor.
So will I turn her virtue into pitch,
And out of her own goodness make the net
That shall enmesh them all.

Re-enter RODERIGO

How now, Roderigo!

RODERIGO

I do follow here in the chase, not like a hound
that hunts, but one that fills up the cry. My
money is almost spent; I have been to-night
exceedingly well cudgelled; and I think the
issue will be, I shall have so much experience
for my pains, and so, with no money at all and
a little more wit, return again to Venice.

IAGO

How poor are they that have not patience!
What wound did ever heal but by degrees?
Thou know'st we work by wit, and not by
    witchcraft;
And wit depends on dilatory time.
Does't not go well? Cassio hath beaten thee.
And thou, by that small hurt, hast cashier'd
    Cassio:
Though other things grow fair against the sun,
Yet fruits that blossom first will first be ripe:
Content thyself awhile. By the mass, 'tis
    morning;
Pleasure and action make the hours seem short.
Retire thee; go where thou art billeted:
Away, I say; thou shalt know more hereafter:
Nay, get thee gone.

Two things are to be done:
My wife must move for Cassio to her mistress;
I'll set her on;
Myself the while to draw the Moor apart,
And bring him jump when he may Cassio find
Soliciting his wife: ay, that's the way
Dull not device by coldness and delay.

Exit

Act III

SCENE I. BEFORE THE CASTLE.

Enter CASSIO and some Musicians

CASSIO

Masters, play here; I will content your pains;
Something that's brief; and bid 'Good morrow,
general.'
Music

Enter Clown

CLOWN

Why masters, have your instruments been in
Naples, that they speak i' the nose thus?

FIRST MUSICIAN

How, sir, how!

CLOWN

Are these, I pray you, wind-instruments?

FIRST MUSICIAN

Ay, marry, are they, sir.

CLOWN

O, thereby hangs a tail.

FIRST MUSICIAN

Whereby hangs a tale, sir?

CLOWN

Marry. Sir, by many a wind-instrument that I know. But, masters, here's money for you: and the general so likes your music, that he desires you, for love's sake, to make no more noise with it.

FIRST MUSICIAN

Well, sir, we will not.

CLOWN

If you have any music that may not be heard, to't again: but, as they say to hear music the general does not greatly care.

FIRST MUSICIAN

We have none such, sir.

CLOWN

Then put up your pipes in your bag, for I'll away: go; vanish into air; away!

Exeunt Musicians

CASSIO

Dost thou hear, my honest friend?

CLOWN

No, I hear not your honest friend; I hear you.

CASSIO

> Prithee, keep up thy quillets. There's a poor
> piece of gold for thee: if the gentlewoman that
> attends the general's wife be stirring, tell her
> there's one Cassio entreats her a little favour of
> speech: wilt thou do this?

CLOWN

> She is stirring, sir: if she will stir hither, I shall
> seem to notify unto her.

CASSIO

> Do, good my friend.

Exit Clown

Enter IAGO

> In happy time, Iago.

IAGO

> You have not been abed, then?

CASSIO

> Why, no; the day had broke
> Before we parted. I have made bold, Iago,
> To send in to your wife: my suit to her
> Is, that she will to virtuous Desdemona
> Procure me some access.

IAGO

> I'll send her to you presently;
> And I'll devise a mean to draw the Moor
> Out of the way, that your converse and business
> May be more free.

93

CASSIO

I humbly thank you for't.

Exit IAGO

I never knew
A Florentine more kind and honest.

Enter EMILIA

EMILIA

Good morrow, good Lieutenant: I am sorry
For your displeasure; but all will sure be well.
The general and his wife are talking of it;
And she speaks for you stoutly: the Moor replies,
That he you hurt is of great fame in Cyprus,
And great affinity, and that in wholesome wisdom
He might not but refuse you; but he protests he loves you
And needs no other suitor but his likings
To take the safest occasion by the front
To bring you in again.

CASSIO

Yet, I beseech you,
If you think fit, or that it may be done,
Give me advantage of some brief discourse
With Desdemona alone.

EMILIA

    Pray you, come in;

    I will bestow you where you shall have time

    To speak your bosom freely.

CASSIO

    I am much bound to you.

Exeunt

SCENE II. A ROOM IN THE CASTLE.

Enter OTHELLO, IAGO, and Gentlemen

OTHELLO

    These letters give, Iago, to the pilot;

    And by him do my duties to the senate:

    That done, I will be walking on the works;

    Repair there to me.

IAGO

    Well, my good lord, I'll do't.

OTHELLO

    This fortification, gentlemen, shall we see't?

GENTLEMAN

    We'll wait upon your lordship.

Exeunt

SCENE III. THE GARDEN
OF THE CASTLE.

Enter DESDEMONA, CASSIO, and EMILIA

DESDEMONA

Be thou assured, good Cassio, I will do
All my abilities in thy behalf.

EMILIA

Good madam, do: I warrant it grieves my
husband,
As if the case were his.

DESDEMONA

O, that's an honest fellow. Do not doubt,
Cassio,
But I will have my lord and you again
As friendly as you were.

CASSIO

Bounteous madam,
Whatever shall become of Michael Cassio,
He's never any thing but your true servant.

DESDEMONA

I know't; I thank you. You do love my lord:
You have known him long; and be you well
assured
He shall in strangeness stand no further off
Than in a politic distance.

CASSIO

> Ay, but, lady,
> That policy may either last so long,
> Or feed upon such nice and waterish diet,
> Or breed itself so out of circumstance,
> That, I being absent and my place supplied,
> My general will forget my love and service.

DESDEMONA

> Do not doubt that; before Emilia here
> I give thee warrant of thy place: assure thee,
> If I do vow a friendship, I'll perform it
> To the last article: my lord shall never rest;
> I'll watch him tame and talk him out of
>   patience;
> His bed shall seem a school, his board a shrift;
> I'll intermingle every thing he does
> With Cassio's suit: therefore be merry, Cassio;
> For thy solicitor shall rather die
> Than give thy cause away.

EMILIA

> Madam, here comes my lord.

CASSIO

> Madam, I'll take my leave.

DESDEMONA

> Why, stay, and hear me speak.

CASSIO

Madam, not now: I am very ill at ease,
Unfit for mine own purposes.

DESDEMONA

Well, do your discretion.

Exit CASSIO

Enter OTHELLO and IAGO

IAGO

Ha! I like not that.

OTHELLO

What dost thou say?

IAGO

Nothing, my lord: or if—I know not what.

OTHELLO

Was not that Cassio parted from my wife?

IAGO

Cassio, my lord! No, sure, I cannot think it,
That he would sneak away so guilty-like,
Seeing you coming.

OTHELLO

I do believe 'twas he.

DESDEMONA

How now, my lord!
I have been talking with a suitor here,
A man that languishes in your displeasure.

OTHELLO

Who is't you mean?

DESDEMONA

Why, your lieutenant, Cassio. Good my lord,
If I have any grace or power to move you,
His present reconciliation take;
For if he be not one that truly loves you,
That errs in ignorance and not in cunning,
I have no judgment in an honest face:
I prithee, call him back.

OTHELLO

Went he hence now?

DESDEMONA

Ay, sooth; so humbled
That he hath left part of his grief with me,
To suffer with him. Good love, call him back.

OTHELLO

Not now, sweet Desdemona; some other time.

DESDEMONA

But shall't be shortly?

OTHELLO

The sooner, sweet, for you.

DESDEMONA

Shall't be to-night at supper?

OTHELLO

No, not to-night.

DESDEMONA

　　To-morrow dinner, then?

OTHELLO

　　I shall not dine at home;

　　I meet the captains at the citadel.

DESDEMONA

　　Why, then, to-morrow night; or Tuesday morn;

　　On Tuesday noon, or night; on Wednesday
　　　　morn:

　　I prithee, name the time, but let it not

　　Exceed three days: in faith, he's penitent;

　　And yet his trespass, in our common reason—

　　Save that, they say, the wars must make
　　　　examples

　　Out of their best—is not almost a fault

　　To incur a private check. When shall he come?

　　Tell me, Othello: I wonder in my soul,

　　What you would ask me, that I should deny,

　　Or stand so mammering on. What! Michael
　　　　Cassio,

　　That came a-wooing with you, and so many a
　　　　time,

　　When I have spoke of you dispraisingly,

　　Hath ta'en your part; to have so much to do

　　To bring him in! Trust me, I could do much—

OTHELLO

Prithee, no more: let him come when he will;
I will deny thee nothing.

DESDEMONA

Why, this is not a boon;
'Tis as I should entreat you wear your gloves,
Or feed on nourishing dishes, or keep you warm,
Or sue to you to do a peculiar profit
To your own person: nay, when I have a suit
Wherein I mean to touch your love indeed,
It shall be full of poise and difficult weight
And fearful to be granted.

OTHELLO

I will deny thee nothing:
Whereon, I do beseech thee, grant me this,
To leave me but a little to myself.

DESDEMONA

Shall I deny you? No: farewell, my lord.

OTHELLO

Farewell, my Desdemona: I'll come to thee
straight.

DESDEMONA

Emilia, come. Be as your fancies teach you;
Whate'er you be, I am obedient.

Exeunt DESDEMONA and
EMILIA

OTHELLO

Excellent wretch! Perdition catch my soul,
But I do love thee! and when I love thee not,
Chaos is come again.

IAGO

My noble lord—

OTHELLO

What dost thou say, Iago?

IAGO

Did Michael Cassio, when you woo'd my lady,
Know of your love?

OTHELLO

He did, from first to last: why dost thou ask?

IAGO

But for a satisfaction of my thought;
No further harm.

OTHELLO

Why of thy thought, Iago?

IAGO

I did not think he had been acquainted with
her.

OTHELLO

O, yes; and went between us very oft.

IAGO

Indeed!

OTHELLO

Indeed! ay, indeed: discern'st thou aught in that?

Is he not honest?

IAGO

Honest, my lord!

OTHELLO

Honest! ay, honest.

IAGO

My lord, for aught I know.

OTHELLO

What dost thou think?

IAGO

Think, my lord!

OTHELLO

Think, my lord!

By heaven, he echoes me,

As if there were some monster in his thought

Too hideous to be shown. Thou dost mean something:

I heard thee say even now, thou likedst not that,

When Cassio left my wife: what didst not like?

And when I told thee he was of my counsel

In my whole course of wooing, thou criedst 'Indeed!'

And didst contract and purse thy brow together,

As if thou then hadst shut up in thy brain

Some horrible conceit: if thou dost love me,
Show me thy thought.

IAGO

My lord, you know I love you.

OTHELLO

I think thou dost;
And, for I know thou'rt full of love and
honesty,
And weigh'st thy words before thou givest
them breath,
Therefore these stops of thine fright me the
more:
For such things in a false disloyal knave
Are tricks of custom, but in a man that's just
They are close delations, working from the
heart
That passion cannot rule.

IAGO

For Michael Cassio,
I dare be sworn I think that he is honest.

OTHELLO

I think so too.

IAGO

Men should be what they seem;
Or those that be not, would they might seem
none!

OTHELLO

Certain, men should be what they seem.

IAGO

Why, then, I think Cassio's an honest man.

OTHELLO

Nay, yet there's more in this:

I prithee, speak to me as to thy thinkings,

As thou dost ruminate, and give thy worst of
thoughts

The worst of words.

IAGO

Good my lord, pardon me:

Though I am bound to every act of duty,

I am not bound to that all slaves are free to.

Utter my thoughts? Why, say they are vile and
false;

As where's that palace whereinto foul things

Sometimes intrude not? Who has a breast so
pure,

But some uncleanly apprehensions

Keep leets and law-days and in session sit

With meditations lawful?

OTHELLO

Thou dost conspire against thy friend, Iago,

If thou but think'st him wrong'd and makest
his ear

A stranger to thy thoughts.

IAGO

I do beseech you—
Though I perchance am vicious in my guess,
As, I confess, it is my nature's plague
To spy into abuses, and oft my jealousy
Shapes faults that are not—that your wisdom yet,
From one that so imperfectly conceits,
Would take no notice, nor build yourself a trouble
Out of his scattering and unsure observance.
It were not for your quiet nor your good,
Nor for my manhood, honesty, or wisdom,
To let you know my thoughts.

OTHELLO

Zounds! What dost thou mean?

IAGO

Good name in man and woman, dear my lord,
Is the immediate jewel of their souls:
Who steals my purse steals trash; 'tis something, nothing;
'Twas mine, 'tis his, and has been slave to thousands:
But he that filches from me my good name
Robs me of that which not enriches him
And makes me poor indeed.

OTHELLO
    By heaven, I'll know thy thoughts.
IAGO
    You cannot, if my heart were in your hand;
    Nor shall not, whilst 'tis in my custody.
OTHELLO
    Ha!
IAGO
    O, beware, my lord, of jealousy;
    It is the green-eyed monster which doth mock
    The meat it feeds on; that cuckold lives in bliss
    Who, certain of his fate, loves not his wronger;
    But, O, what damned minutes tells he o'er
    Who dotes, yet doubts, suspects, yet strongly
        loves!
OTHELLO
    O misery!
IAGO
    Poor and content is rich and rich enough,
    But riches fineless is as poor as winter
    To him that ever fears he shall be poor.
    Good heaven, the souls of all my tribe defend
    From jealousy!
OTHELLO
    Why, why is this?
    Think'st thou I'd make a lie of jealousy,

To follow still the changes of the moon
With fresh suspicions? No; to be once in doubt
Is once to be resolved: exchange me for a goat,
When I shall turn the business of my soul
To such exsufflicate and blown surmises,
Matching thy inference. 'Tis not to make me
    jealous
To say my wife is fair, feeds well, loves company,
Is free of speech, sings, plays and dances well;
Where virtue is, these are more virtuous:
Nor from mine own weak merits will I draw
The smallest fear or doubt of her revolt;
For she had eyes, and chose me. No, Iago;
I'll see before I doubt; when I doubt, prove;
And on the proof, there is no more but this—
Away at once with love or jealousy!

IAGO

I am glad of it; for now I shall have reason
To show the love and duty that I bear you
With franker spirit: therefore, as I am bound,
Receive it from me. I speak not yet of proof.
Look to your wife; observe her well with Cassio;
Wear your eye thus, not jealous nor secure:
I would not have your free and noble nature,
Out of self-bounty, be abused; look to't:
I know our country disposition well;

In Venice they do let heaven see the pranks
They dare not show their husbands; their best
    conscience
Is not to leave't undone, but keep't unknown.

OTHELLO

Dost thou say so?

IAGO

She did deceive her father, marrying you;
And when she seem'd to shake and fear your
    looks,
She loved them most.

OTHELLO

And so she did.

IAGO

Why, go to then;
She that, so young, could give out such a
    seeming,
To seal her father's eyes up close as oak-
He thought 'twas witchcraft—but I am much
    to blame;
I humbly do beseech you of your pardon
For too much loving you.

OTHELLO

I am bound to thee for ever.

IAGO

I see this hath a little dash'd your spirits.

OTHELLO

Not a jot, not a jot.

IAGO

I' faith, I fear it has.

I hope you will consider what is spoke

Comes from my love. But I do see you're
moved:

I am to pray you not to strain my speech

To grosser issues nor to larger reach

Than to suspicion.

OTHELLO

I will not.

IAGO

Should you do so, my lord,

My speech should fall into such vile success

As my thoughts aim not at. Cassio's my worthy
friend—

My lord, I see you're moved.

OTHELLO

No, not much moved:

I do not think but Desdemona's honest.

IAGO

Long live she so! and long live you to think so!

OTHELLO

And yet, how nature erring from itself—

IAGO

Ay, there's the point: as—to be bold with you—

Not to affect many proposed matches
Of her own clime, complexion, and degree,
Whereto we see in all things nature tends—
Foh! one may smell in such a will most rank,
Foul disproportion thoughts unnatural.
But pardon me; I do not in position
Distinctly speak of her; though I may fear
Her will, recoiling to her better judgment,
May fall to match you with her country forms
And happily repent.

OTHELLO

Farewell, farewell:
If more thou dost perceive, let me know more;
Set on thy wife to observe: leave me, Iago:

IAGO

[*Going*] My lord, I take my leave.

OTHELLO

Why did I marry? This honest creature
doubtless
Sees and knows more, much more, than he
unfolds.

IAGO

[*Returning*] My lord, I would I might entreat
your honour
To scan this thing no further; leave it to time:
Though it be fit that Cassio have his place,
For sure, he fills it up with great ability,

Yet, if you please to hold him off awhile,
You shall by that perceive him and his means:
Note, if your lady strain his entertainment
With any strong or vehement importunity;
Much will be seen in that. In the mean time,
Let me be thought too busy in my fears—
As worthy cause I have to fear I am—
And hold her free, I do beseech your honour.

OTHELLO

Fear not my government.

IAGO

I once more take my leave.

Exit

OTHELLO

This fellow's of exceeding honesty,
And knows all qualities, with a learned spirit,
Of human dealings. If I do prove her haggard,
Though that her jesses were my dear
    heartstrings,
I'd whistle her off and let her down the wind,
To pray at fortune. Haply, for I am black
And have not those soft parts of conversation
That chamberers have, or for I am declined
Into the vale of years—yet that's not much—
She's gone. I am abused; and my relief
Must be to loathe her. O curse of marriage,
That we can call these delicate creatures ours,

And not their appetites! I had rather be a toad,
And live upon the vapour of a dungeon,
Than keep a corner in the thing I love
For others' uses. Yet, 'tis the plague of great ones;
Prerogatived are they less than the base;
'Tis destiny unshunnable, like death:
Even then this forked plague is fated to us
When we do quicken. Desdemona comes:

Re-enter DESDEMONA and

EMILIA

If she be false, O, then heaven mocks itself!
I'll not believe it.

DESDEMONA

How now, my dear Othello?
Your dinner, and the generous islanders
By you invited, do attend your presence.

OTHELLO

I am to blame.

DESDEMONA

Why do you speak so faintly?
Are you not well?

OTHELLO

I have a pain upon my forehead here.

DESDEMONA

Faith, that's with watching; 'twill away again:
Let me but bind it hard, within this hour
It will be well.

113

OTHELLO

 Your napkin is too little:

 He puts the handkerchief from him; and it drops

 Let it alone. Come, I'll go in with you.

DESDEMONA

 I am very sorry that you are not well.

       Exeunt OTHELLO and

         DESDEMONA

EMILIA

 I am glad I have found this napkin:

 This was her first remembrance from the Moor:

 My wayward husband hath a hundred times

 Woo'd me to steal it; but she so loves the token,

 For he conjured her she should ever keep it,

 That she reserves it evermore about her

 To kiss and talk to. I'll have the work ta'en out,

 And give't Iago: what he will do with it

 Heaven knows, not I;

 I nothing but to please his fantasy.

     Re-enter IAGO

IAGO

 How now! what do you here alone?

EMILIA

 Do not you chide; I have a thing for you.

IAGO

 A thing for me? It is a common thing—

EMILIA

Ha!

IAGO

To have a foolish wife.

EMILIA

O, is that all? What will you give me now

For the same handkerchief?

IAGO

What handkerchief?

EMILIA

What handkerchief?

Why, that the Moor first gave to Desdemona;

That which so often you did bid me steal.

IAGO

Hast stol'n it from her?

EMILIA

No, 'faith; she let it drop by negligence.

And, to the advantage, I, being here, took't up.

Look, here it is.

IAGO

A good wench; give it me.

EMILIA

What will you do with't, that you have been so

earnest

To have me filch it?

IAGO

[*Snatching it*] Why, what's that to you?

EMILIA

If it be not for some purpose of import,
Give't me again: poor lady, she'll run mad
When she shall lack it.

IAGO

Be not acknown on't; I have use for it.
Go, leave me.

Exit EMILIA

I will in Cassio's lodging lose this napkin,
And let him find it. Trifles light as air
Are to the jealous confirmations strong
As proofs of holy writ: this may do something.
The Moor already changes with my poison:
Dangerous conceits are, in their natures,
    poisons.
Which at the first are scarce found to distaste,
But with a little act upon the blood.
Burn like the mines of Sulphur. I did say so:
Look, where he comes!

Re-enter OTHELLO

Not poppy, nor mandragora,
Nor all the drowsy syrups of the world,
Shall ever medicine thee to that sweet sleep
Which thou owedst yesterday.

OTHELLO

Ha! ha! false to me, to me?

IAGO

Why, how now, general! no more of that.

OTHELLO

Avaunt! be gone! thou hast set me on the rack:

I swear 'tis better to be much abused

Than but to know't a little.

IAGO

How now, my lord!

OTHELLO

What sense had I of her stol'n hours of lust?

I saw't not, thought it not, it harm'd not me:

I slept the next night well, was free and merry;

I found not Cassio's kisses on her lips:

He that is robb'd, not wanting what is stol'n,

Let him not know't, and he's not robb'd at all.

IAGO

I am sorry to hear this.

OTHELLO

I had been happy, if the general camp,

Pioners and all, had tasted her sweet body,

So I had nothing known. O, now, for ever

Farewell the tranquil mind! farewell content!

Farewell the plumed troop, and the big wars,

That make ambition virtue! O, farewell!

Farewell the neighing steed, and the shrill

trump,

The spirit-stirring drum, the ear-piercing fife,
The royal banner, and all quality,
Pride, pomp and circumstance of glorious war!
And, O you mortal engines, whose rude throats
The immortal Jove's dead clamours counterfeit,
Farewell! Othello's occupation's gone!

IAGO

Is't possible, my lord?

OTHELLO

Villain, be sure thou prove my love a whore,
   Taking him by the throat
Be sure of it; give me the ocular proof:
Or by the worth of man's eternal soul,
Thou hadst been better have been born a dog
Than answer my waked wrath!

IAGO

Is't come to this?

OTHELLO

Make me to see't; or, at the least, so prove it,
That the probation bear no hinge nor loop
To hang a doubt on; or woe upon thy life!

IAGO

My noble lord—

OTHELLO

If thou dost slander her and torture me,
Never pray more; abandon all remorse;
On horror's head horrors accumulate;

Do deeds to make heaven weep, all earth amazed;
For nothing canst thou to damnation add
Greater than that.

IAGO

O grace! O heaven forgive me!
Are you a man? Have you a soul or sense?
God be wi' you; take mine office. O wretched
   fool.
That livest to make thine honesty a vice!
O monstrous world! Take note, take note, O
   world,
To be direct and honest is not safe.
I thank you for this profit; and from hence
I'll love no friend, sith love breeds such offence.

OTHELLO

Nay, stay: thou shouldst be honest.

IAGO

I should be wise, for honesty's a fool
And loses that it works for.

OTHELLO

By the world,
I think my wife be honest and think she is not;
I think that thou art just and think thou art not.
I'll have some proof. Her name, that was as
   fresh
As Dian's visage, is now begrimed and black
As mine own face. If there be cords, or knives,

Poison, or fire, or suffocating streams,
I'll not endure it. Would I were satisfied!

IAGO

I see, sir, you are eaten up with passion:
I do repent me that I put it to you.
You would be satisfied?

OTHELLO

Would! nay, I will.

IAGO

And may: but, how? How satisfied, my lord?
Would you, the supervisor, grossly gape on—
Behold her topp'd?

OTHELLO

Death and damnation! O!

IAGO

It were a tedious difficulty, I think,
To bring them to that prospect: damn them then,
If ever mortal eyes do see them bolster
More than their own! What then? how then?
What shall I say? Where's satisfaction?
It is impossible you should see this,
Were they as prime as goats, as hot as monkeys,
As salt as wolves in pride, and fools as gross
As ignorance made drunk. But yet, I say,
If imputation and strong circumstances,
Which lead directly to the door of truth,
Will give you satisfaction, you may have't.

OTHELLO

Give me a living reason she's disloyal.

IAGO

I do not like the office:
But, sith I am enter'd in this cause so far,
Prick'd to't by foolish honesty and love,
I will go on. I lay with Cassio lately;
And, being troubled with a raging tooth,
I could not sleep.
There are a kind of men so loose of soul,
That in their sleeps will mutter their affairs:
One of this kind is Cassio:
In sleep I heard him say 'Sweet Desdemona,
Let us be wary, let us hide our loves;'
And then, sir, would he gripe and wring my hand,
Cry 'O sweet creature!' and then kiss me hard,
As if he pluck'd up kisses by the roots
That grew upon my lips: then laid his leg
Over my thigh, and sigh'd, and kiss'd; and then
Cried 'Cursed fate that gave thee to the Moor!'

OTHELLO

O monstrous! monstrous!

IAGO

Nay, this was but his dream.

OTHELLO

But this denoted a foregone conclusion:
'Tis a shrewd doubt, though it be but a dream.

IAGO

And this may help to thicken other proofs
That do demonstrate thinly.

OTHELLO

I'll tear her all to pieces.

IAGO

Nay, but be wise: yet we see nothing done;
She may be honest yet. Tell me but this,
Have you not sometimes seen a handkerchief
Spotted with strawberries in your wife's hand?

OTHELLO

I gave her such a one; 'twas my first gift.

IAGO

I know not that; but such a handkerchief—
I am sure it was your wife's—did I to-day
See Cassio wipe his beard with.

OTHELLO

If it be that—

IAGO

If it be that, or any that was hers,
It speaks against her with the other proofs.

OTHELLO

O, that the slave had forty thousand lives!
One is too poor, too weak for my revenge.
Now do I see 'tis true. Look here, Iago;
All my fond love thus do I blow to heaven.
'Tis gone.

Arise, black vengeance, from thy hollow hell!
Yield up, O love, thy crown and hearted throne
To tyrannous hate! Swell, bosom, with thy
    fraught,
For 'tis of aspics' tongues!

IAGO

Yet be content.

OTHELLO

O, blood, blood, blood!

IAGO

Patience, I say; your mind perhaps may change.

OTHELLO

Never, Iago: Like to the Pontic sea,
Whose icy current and compulsive course
Ne'er feels retiring ebb, but keeps due on
To the Propontic and the Hellespont,
Even so my bloody thoughts, with violent pace,
Shall ne'er look back, ne'er ebb to humble love,
Till that a capable and wide revenge
Swallow them up. Now, by yond marble heaven,

Kneels

In the due reverence of a sacred vow
I here engage my words.

IAGO

Do not rise yet.

Kneels

Witness, you ever-burning lights above,

123

You elements that clip us round about,
Witness that here Iago doth give up
The execution of his wit, hands, heart,
To wrong'd Othello's service! Let him command,
And to obey shall be in me remorse,
What bloody business ever.

They rise

OTHELLO

I greet thy love,
Not with vain thanks, but with acceptance bounteous,
And will upon the instant put thee to't:
Within these three days let me hear thee say
That Cassio's not alive.

IAGO

My friend is dead; 'tis done at your request:
But let her live.

OTHELLO

Damn her, lewd minx! O, damn her!
Come, go with me apart; I will withdraw,
To furnish me with some swift means of death
For the fair devil. Now art thou my lieutenant.

IAGO

I am your own for ever.

Exeunt

SCENE IV. BEFORE THE CASTLE.

Enter DESDEMONA, EMILIA, and CLOWN

DESDEMONA

Do you know, sirrah, where Lieutenant Cassio lies?

CLOWN

I dare not say he lies any where.

DESDEMONA

Why, man?

CLOWN

He's a soldier, and for one to say a soldier lies, 'tis stabbing.

DESDEMONA

Go to: where lodges he?

CLOWN

To tell you where he lodges, is to tell you where I lie.

DESDEMONA

Can any thing be made of this?

CLOWN

I know not where he lodges, and for me to devise a lodging and say he lies here or he lies there, were to lie in mine own throat.

DESDEMONA

Can you inquire him out, and be edified by report?

CLOWN

I will catechise the world for him; that is, make
questions, and by them answer.

DESDEMONA

Seek him, bid him come hither: tell him I have
moved my lord on his behalf, and hope all will
be well.

CLOWN

To do this is within the compass of man's wit:
and therefore I will attempt the doing it.

Exit

DESDEMONA

Where should I lose that handkerchief, Emilia?

EMILIA

I know not, madam.

DESDEMONA

Believe me, I had rather have lost my purse
Full of crusadoes: and, but my noble Moor
Is true of mind and made of no such baseness
As jealous creatures are, it were enough
To put him to ill thinking.

EMILIA

Is he not jealous?

DESDEMONA

Who, he? I think the sun where he was born
Drew all such humours from him.

EMILIA

Look, where he comes.

DESDEMONA

I will not leave him now till Cassio
Be call'd to him.

Enter OTHELLO

How is't with you, my lord?

OTHELLO

Well, my good lady.

Aside

O, hardness to dissemble!—
How do you, Desdemona?

DESDEMONA

Well, my good lord.

OTHELLO

Give me your hand: this hand is moist, my lady.

DESDEMONA

It yet hath felt no age nor known no sorrow.

OTHELLO

This argues fruitfulness and liberal heart:
Hot, hot, and moist: this hand of yours requires
A sequester from liberty, fasting and prayer,
Much castigation, exercise devout;
For here's a young and sweating devil here,
That commonly rebels. 'Tis a good hand,
A frank one.

DESDEMONA

You may, indeed, say so;

For 'twas that hand that gave away my heart.

OTHELLO

A liberal hand: the hearts of old gave hands;

But our new heraldry is hands, not hearts.

DESDEMONA

I cannot speak of this. Come now, your promise.

OTHELLO

What promise, chuck?

DESDEMONA

I have sent to bid Cassio come speak with you.

OTHELLO

I have a salt and sorry rheum offends me;

Lend me thy handkerchief.

DESDEMONA

Here, my lord.

OTHELLO

That which I gave you.

DESDEMONA

I have it not about me.

OTHELLO

Not?

DESDEMONA

No, indeed, my lord.

OTHELLO

That is a fault.

That handkerchief
Did an Egyptian to my mother give;
She was a charmer, and could almost read
The thoughts of people: she told her, while she
    kept it,
'Twould make her amiable and subdue my father
Entirely to her love, but if she lost it
Or made gift of it, my father's eye
Should hold her loathed and his spirits should
    hunt
After new fancies: she, dying, gave it me;
And bid me, when my fate would have me wive,
To give it her. I did so: and take heed on't;
Make it a darling like your precious eye;
To lose't or give't away were such perdition
As nothing else could match.

DESDEMONA

Is't possible?

OTHELLO

'Tis true: there's magic in the web of it:
A sibyl, that had number'd in the world
The sun to course two hundred compasses,
In her prophetic fury sew'd the work;
The worms were hallow'd that did breed
    the silk;
And it was dyed in mummy which the skilful
Conserved of maidens' hearts.

DESDEMONA

Indeed! is't true?

OTHELLO

Most veritable; therefore look to't well.

DESDEMONA

Then would to God that I had never seen't!

OTHELLO

Ha! wherefore?

DESDEMONA

Why do you speak so startingly and rash?

OTHELLO

Is't lost? Is't gone? Speak, is it out o' the way?

DESDEMONA

Heaven bless us!

OTHELLO

Say you?

DESDEMONA

It is not lost; but what an if it were?

OTHELLO

How!

DESDEMONA

I say, it is not lost.

OTHELLO

Fetch't, let me see't.

DESDEMONA

Why, so I can, sir, but I will not now.

This is a trick to put me from my suit:
Pray you, let Cassio be received again.

OTHELLO

Fetch me the handkerchief: my mind misgives.

DESDEMONA

Come, come;
You'll never meet a more sufficient man.

OTHELLO

The handkerchief!

DESDEMONA

I pray, talk me of Cassio.

OTHELLO

The handkerchief!

DESDEMONA

A man that all his time
Hath founded his good fortunes on your love,
Shared dangers with you—

OTHELLO

The handkerchief!

DESDEMONA

I'faith, you are to blame.

OTHELLO

Away!

Exit

EMILIA

Is not this man jealous?

DESDEMONA

    I ne'er saw this before.

    Sure, there's some wonder in this handkerchief:

    I am most unhappy in the loss of it.

EMILIA

    'Tis not a year or two shows us a man:

    They are all but stomachs, and we all but food;

    To eat us hungerly, and when they are full,

    They belch us. Look you, Cassio and my

        husband!

Enter CASSIO and IAGO

IAGO

    There is no other way; 'tis she must do't:

    And, lo, the happiness! go, and importune her.

DESDEMONA

    How now, good Cassio! what's the news with

    you?

CASSIO

    Madam, my former suit: I do beseech you

    That by your virtuous means I may again

    Exist, and be a member of his love

    Whom I with all the office of my heart

    Entirely honour: I would not be delay'd.

    If my offence be of such mortal kind

    That nor my service past, nor present sorrows,

    Nor purposed merit in futurity,

    Can ransom me into his love again,

But to know so must be my benefit;
So shall I clothe me in a forced content,
And shut myself up in some other course,
To fortune's alms.

DESDEMONA

Alas, thrice-gentle Cassio!
My advocation is not now in tune;
My lord is not my lord; nor should I know him,
Were he in favour as in humour alter'd.
So help me every spirit sanctified,
As I have spoken for you all my best
And stood within the blank of his displeasure
For my free speech! you must awhile be patient:
What I can do I will; and more I will
Than for myself I dare: let that suffice you.

IAGO

Is my lord angry?

EMILIA

He went hence but now,
And certainly in strange unquietness.

IAGO

Can he be angry? I have seen the cannon,
When it hath blown his ranks into the air,
And, like the devil, from his very arm
Puff'd his own brother:—and can he be angry?
Something of moment then: I will go meet him:
There's matter in't indeed, if he be angry.

DESDEMONA

    I prithee, do so.

Exit IAGO

    Something, sure, of state,
    Either from Venice, or some unhatch'd practise
    Made demonstrable here in Cyprus to him,
    Hath puddled his clear spirit: and in such cases
    Men's natures wrangle with inferior things,
    Though great ones are their object. 'Tis even so;
    For let our finger ache, and it endues
    Our other healthful members even to that sense
    Of pain: nay, we must think men are not gods,
    Nor of them look for such observances
    As fit the bridal. Beshrew me much, Emilia,
    I was, unhandsome warrior as I am,
    Arraigning his unkindness with my soul;
    But now I find I had suborn'd the witness,
    And he's indicted falsely.

EMILIA

    Pray heaven it be state-matters, as you think,
    And no conception nor no jealous toy
    Concerning you.

DESDEMONA

    Alas the day! I never gave him cause.

EMILIA

    But jealous souls will not be answer'd so;

They are not ever jealous for the cause,
But jealous for they are jealous: 'tis a monster
Begot upon itself, born on itself.

DESDEMONA

Heaven keep that monster from Othello's mind!

EMILIA

Lady, amen.

DESDEMONA

I will go seek him. Cassio, walk hereabout:
If I do find him fit, I'll move your suit
And seek to effect it to my uttermost.

CASSIO

I humbly thank your ladyship.

Exeunt DESDEMONA and
EMILIA

Enter BIANCA

BIANCA

Save you, friend Cassio!

CASSIO

What make you from home?
How is it with you, my most fair Bianca?
I' faith, sweet love, I was coming to your house.

BIANCA

And I was going to your lodging, Cassio.
What, keep a week away? Seven days and nights?

Eight score eight hours? And lovers' absent hours,
More tedious than the dial eight score times?
O weary reckoning!

CASSIO

Pardon me, Bianca:
I have this while with leaden thoughts been
press'd:
But I shall, in a more continuate time,
Strike off this score of absence. Sweet Bianca,
Giving her DESDEMONA's handkerchief
Take me this work out.

BIANCA

O Cassio, whence came this?
This is some token from a newer friend:
To the felt absence now I feel a cause:
Is't come to this? Well, well.

CASSIO

Go to, woman!
Throw your vile guesses in the devil's teeth,
From whence you have them. You are jealous
now
That this is from some mistress, some
remembrance:
No, in good troth, Bianca.

BIANCA

Why, whose is it?

CASSIO

    I know not, neither: I found it in my chamber.

    I like the work well: ere it be demanded—

    As like enough it will—I'ld have it copied:

    Take it, and do't; and leave me for this time.

BIANCA

    Leave you! wherefore?

CASSIO

    I do attend here on the general;

    And think it no addition, nor my wish,

    To have him see me woman'd.

BIANCA

    Why, I pray you?

CASSIO

    Not that I love you not.

BIANCA

    But that you do not love me.

    I pray you, bring me on the way a little,

    And say if I shall see you soon at night.

CASSIO

    'Tis but a little way that I can bring you;

    For I attend here: but I'll see you soon.

BIANCA

    'Tis very good; I must be circumstanced.

Exeunt

Act IV

SCENE I. CYPRUS. BEFORE THE CASTLE.

Enter OTHELLO and IAGO

IAGO

Will you think so?

OTHELLO

Think so, Iago!

IAGO

What,

To kiss in private?

OTHELLO

An unauthorized kiss.

IAGO

Or to be naked with her friend in bed

An hour or more, not meaning any harm?

OTHELLO

Naked in bed, Iago, and not mean harm!

It is hypocrisy against the devil:

They that mean virtuously, and yet do so,
The devil their virtue tempts, and they tempt
    heaven.

IAGO

So they do nothing, 'tis a venial slip:
But if I give my wife a handkerchief—

OTHELLO

What then?

IAGO

Why, then, 'tis hers, my lord; and, being hers,
She may, I think, bestow't on any man.

OTHELLO

She is protectress of her honour too:
May she give that?

IAGO

Her honour is an essence that's not seen;
They have it very oft that have it not:
But, for the handkerchief—

OTHELLO

By heaven, I would most gladly have forgot it.
Thou said'st, it comes o'er my memory,
As doth the raven o'er the infected house,
Boding to all—he had my handkerchief.

IAGO

Ay, what of that?

OTHELLO

That's not so good now.

IAGO

What,
If I had said I had seen him do you wrong?
Or heard him say—as knaves be such abroad,
Who having, by their own importunate suit,
Or voluntary dotage of some mistress,
Convinced or supplied them, cannot choose
But they must blab—

OTHELLO

Hath he said any thing?

IAGO

He hath, my lord; but be you well assured,
No more than he'll unswear.

OTHELLO

What hath he said?

IAGO

'Faith, that he did—I know not what he did.

OTHELLO

What? what?

IAGO

Lie—

OTHELLO

With her?

IAGO

With her, on her; what you will.

OTHELLO

Lie with her! lie on her! We say lie on her, when

they belie her. Lie with her! that's fulsome. Handkerchief—confessions—handkerchief!—To confess, and be hanged for his labour—first, to be hanged, and then to confess. I tremble at it. Nature would not invest herself in such shadowing passion without some instruction. It is not words that shake me thus. Pish! Noses, ears, and lips. Is't possible? Confess—handkerchief!—O devil!—

Falls in a trance

IAGO

Work on,

My medicine, work! Thus credulous fools are
    caught;

And many worthy and chaste dames even thus,

All guiltless, meet reproach. What, ho! my lord!

My lord, I say! Othello!

Enter CASSIO

How now, Cassio!

CASSIO

What's the matter?

IAGO

My lord is fall'n into an epilepsy:

This is his second fit; he had one yesterday.

CASSIO

Rub him about the temples.

IAGO

No, forbear;

The lethargy must have his quiet course:

If not, he foams at mouth and by and by

Breaks out to savage madness. Look he stirs:

Do you withdraw yourself a little while,

He will recover straight: when he is gone,

I would on great occasion speak with you.

Exit CASSIO

How is it, general? Have you not hurt your head?

OTHELLO

Dost thou mock me?

IAGO

I mock you! no, by heaven.

Would you would bear your fortune like a man!

OTHELLO

A horned man's a monster and a beast.

IAGO

There's many a beast then in a populous city,

And many a civil monster.

OTHELLO

Did he confess it?

IAGO

Good sir, be a man;

Think every bearded fellow that's but yoked

May draw with you: there's millions now alive

That nightly lie in those unproper beds

Which they dare swear peculiar: your case is
better.

O, 'tis the spite of hell, the fiend's arch-mock,

To lip a wanton in a secure couch,

And to suppose her chaste! No, let me know;

And knowing what I am, I know what she
shall be.

OTHELLO

O, thou art wise; 'tis certain.

IAGO

Stand you awhile apart;

Confine yourself but in a patient list.

Whilst you were here o'erwhelmed with your
grief—

A passion most unsuiting such a man—

Cassio came hither: I shifted him away,

And laid good 'scuse upon your ecstasy,

Bade him anon return and here speak with me;

The which he promised. Do but encave
yourself,

And mark the fleers, the gibes, and notable
scorns,

That dwell in every region of his face;

For I will make him tell the tale anew,

Where, how, how oft, how long ago, and when

He hath, and is again to cope your wife:

I say, but mark his gesture. Marry, patience;
Or I shall say you are all in all in spleen,
And nothing of a man.

OTHELLO

Dost thou hear, Iago?
I will be found most cunning in my patience;
But—dost thou hear?—most bloody.

IAGO

That's not amiss;
But yet keep time in all. Will you withdraw?
OTHELLO retires

Now will I question Cassio of Bianca,
A housewife that by selling her desires
Buys herself bread and clothes: it is a creature
That dotes on Cassio; as 'tis the strumpet's
plague
To beguile many and be beguiled by one:
He, when he hears of her, cannot refrain
From the excess of laughter. Here he comes:
Re-enter CASSIO

As he shall smile, Othello shall go mad;
And his unbookish jealousy must construe
Poor Cassio's smiles, gestures and light behavior,
Quite in the wrong. How do you now, lieutenant?

CASSIO

The worser that you give me the addition
Whose want even kills me.

IAGO

Ply Desdemona well, and you are sure on't.

Speaking lower

Now, if this suit lay in Bianco's power,

How quickly should you speed!

CASSIO

Alas, poor caitiff!

OTHELLO

Look, how he laughs already!

IAGO

I never knew woman love man so.

CASSIO

Alas, poor rogue! I think, i' faith, she loves me.

OTHELLO

Now he denies it faintly, and laughs it out.

IAGO

Do you hear, Cassio?

OTHELLO

Now he importunes him

To tell it o'er: go to; well said, well said.

IAGO

She gives it out that you shall marry hey:

Do you intend it?

CASSIO

Ha, ha, ha!

OTHELLO

Do you triumph, Roman? Do you triumph?

CASSIO

    I marry her! what? a customer! Prithee, bear
    some charity to my wit: do not think it so
    unwholesome. Ha, ha, ha!

OTHELLO

    So, so, so, so: they laugh that win.

IAGO

    'Faith, the cry goes that you shall marry her.

CASSIO

    Prithee, say true.

IAGO

    I am a very villain else.

OTHELLO

    Have you scored me? Well.

CASSIO

    This is the monkey's own giving out: she is
    persuaded I will marry her, out of her own love
    and flattery, not out of my promise.

OTHELLO

    Iago beckons me; now he begins the story.

CASSIO

    She was here even now; she haunts me in
    every place. I was the other day talking on the
    sea-bank with certain Venetians; and thither
    comes the bauble, and, by this hand, she falls
    me thus about my neck—

OTHELLO

Crying 'O dear Cassio!' as it were: his gesture imports it.

CASSIO

So hangs, and lolls, and weeps upon me; so hales, and pulls me: ha, ha, ha!

OTHELLO

Now he tells how she plucked him to my chamber. O, I see that nose of yours, but not that dog I shall throw it to.

CASSIO

Well, I must leave her company.

IAGO

Before me! look, where she comes.

CASSIO

'Tis such another fitchew! marry a perfumed one.

Enter BLANCA

What do you mean by this haunting of me?

BIANCA

Let the devil and his dam haunt you! What did you mean by that same handkerchief you gave me even now? I was a fine fool to take it. I must take out the work?—A likely piece of work, that you should find it in your chamber, and not know who left it there! This is some minx's token, and I must take out the work?

There; give it your hobby-horse: wheresoever
you had it, I'll take out no work on't.

CASSIO

How now, my sweet Bianca! How now! How now!

OTHELLO

By heaven, that should be my handkerchief!

BIANCA

An you'll come to supper to-night, you may;
an you will not, come when you are next
prepared for.

Exit

IAGO

After her, after her.

CASSIO

'Faith, I must; she'll rail in the street else.

IAGO

Will you sup there?

CASSIO

'Faith, I intend so.

IAGO

Well, I may chance to see you; for I would very
fain speak with you.

CASSIO

Prithee, come; will you?

IAGO

Go to; say no more.

Exit CASSIO

OTHELLO

[*Advancing*] How shall I murder him, Iago?
IAGO

Did you perceive how he laughed at his vice?
OTHELLO

O Iago!
IAGO

And did you see the handkerchief?
OTHELLO

Was that mine?
IAGO

Yours by this hand: and to see how he prizes
the foolish woman your wife! she gave it him,
and he hath given it his whore.
OTHELLO

I would have him nine years a-killing.

A fine woman! a fair woman! a sweet woman!
IAGO

Nay, you must forget that.
OTHELLO

Ay, let her rot, and perish, and be damned to-
night; for she shall not live: no, my heart is
turned to stone; I strike it, and it hurts my hand.
O, the world hath not a sweeter creature: she
might lie by an emperor's side and command
him tasks.

IAGO

Nay, that's not your way.

OTHELLO

Hang her! I do but say what she is: so delicate
with her needle: an admirable musician: O! she
will sing the savageness out of a bear: of so
high and plenteous wit and invention:—

IAGO

She's the worse for all this.

OTHELLO

O, a thousand thousand times: and then, of so
gentle a condition!

IAGO

Ay, too gentle.

OTHELLO

Nay, that's certain: but yet the pity of it, Iago!
O Iago, the pity of it, Iago!

IAGO

If you are so fond over her iniquity, give her
patent to offend; for, if it touch not you, it
comes near nobody.

OTHELLO

I will chop her into messes: cuckold me!

IAGO

O, 'tis foul in her.

OTHELLO

With mine officer!

IAGO

That's fouler.

OTHELLO

Get me some poison, Iago; this night: I'll not
expostulate with her, lest her body and beauty
unprovide my mind again: this night, Iago.

IAGO

Do it not with poison, strangle her in her bed,
even the bed she hath contaminated.

OTHELLO

Good, good: the justice of it pleases: very good.

IAGO

And for Cassio, let me be his undertaker: you
shall hear more by midnight.

OTHELLO

Excellent good.

A trumpet within

What trumpet is that same?

IAGO

I warrant, something from Venice, sure. 'Tis
Lodovico Come from the Duke: and, see, your
wife is with him.

Enter LODOVICO,
DESDEMONA, and Attendants

LODOVICO

Save you, worthy general!

OTHELLO

    With all my heart, sir.

LODOVICO

    The Duke and Senators of Venice greet you.

              Gives him a letter

OTHELLO

    I kiss the instrument of their pleasures.

              Opens the letter, and reads

DESDEMONA

    And what's the news, good cousin Lodovico?

IAGO

    I am very glad to see you, signior

    Welcome to Cyprus.

LODOVICO

    I thank you. How does Lieutenant Cassio?

IAGO

    Lives, sir.

DESDEMONA

    Cousin, there's fall'n between him and my lord

    An unkind breach: but you shall make all well.

OTHELLO

    Are you sure of that?

DESDEMONA

    My lord?

OTHELLO

    [*Reads*] 'This fail you not to do, as you will—'

LODOVICO

    He did not call; he's busy in the paper.

    Is there division 'twixt my lord and Cassio?

DESDEMONA

    A most unhappy one: I would do much

    To atone them, for the love I bear to Cassio.

OTHELLO

    Fire and brimstone!

DESDEMONA

    My lord?

OTHELLO

    Are you wise?

DESDEMONA

    What, is he angry?

LODOVICO

    May be the letter moved him;

    For, as I think, they do command him home,

    Deputing Cassio in his government.

DESDEMONA

    Trust me, I am glad on't.

OTHELLO

    Indeed!

DESDEMONA

    My lord?

OTHELLO

    I am glad to see you mad.

DESDEMONA

Why, sweet Othello?

OTHELLO

[*Striking her*] Devil!

DESDEMONA

I have not deserved this.

LODOVICO

My lord, this would not be believed in Venice,

Though I should swear I saw't: 'tis very much:

Make her amends; she weeps.

OTHELLO

O devil, devil!

If that the earth could teem with woman's tears,

Each drop she falls would prove a crocodile.

Out of my sight!

DESDEMONA

I will not stay to offend you.

Going

LODOVICO

Truly, an obedient lady:

I do beseech your lordship, call her back.

OTHELLO

Mistress!

DESDEMONA

My lord?

OTHELLO

What would you with her, sir?

LODOVICO

Who, I, my lord?

OTHELLO

Ay; you did wish that I would make her turn:
Sir, she can turn, and turn, and yet go on,
And turn again; and she can weep, sir, weep;
And she's obedient, as you say, obedient,
Very obedient. Proceed you in your tears.
Concerning this, sir,—O well-painted passion!—
I am commanded home. Get you away;
I'll send for you anon. Sir, I obey the mandate,
And will return to Venice. Hence, avaunt!

Exit DESDEMONA

Cassio shall have my place. And, sir, tonight,
I do entreat that we may sup together:
You are welcome, sir, to Cyprus. Goats and
   monkeys!

Exit

LODOVICO

Is this the noble Moor whom our full Senate
Call all in all sufficient? Is this the nature
Whom passion could not shake? Whose solid
   virtue
The shot of accident, nor dart of chance,
Could neither graze nor pierce?

IAGO

He is much changed.

LODOVICO

Are his wits safe? Is he not light of brain?

IAGO

He's that he is: I may not breathe my censure
What he might be: if what he might he is not,
I would to heaven he were!

LODOVICO

What, strike his wife!

IAGO

'Faith, that was not so well; yet would I knew
That stroke would prove the worst!

LODOVICO

Is it his use?
Or did the letters work upon his blood,
And new-create this fault?

IAGO

Alas, alas!
It is not honesty in me to speak
What I have seen and known. You shall observe
    him,
And his own courses will denote him so
That I may save my speech: do but go after,
And mark how he continues.

LODOVICO

I am sorry that I am deceived in him.

Exeunt

SCENE II. A ROOM IN THE CASTLE.

Enter OTHELLO and EMILIA

OTHELLO

You have seen nothing then?

EMILIA

Nor ever heard, nor ever did suspect.

OTHELLO

Yes, you have seen Cassio and she together.

EMILIA

But then I saw no harm, and then I heard
Each syllable that breath made up between
them.

OTHELLO

What, did they never whisper?

EMILIA

Never, my lord.

OTHELLO

Nor send you out o' the way?

EMILIA

Never.

OTHELLO

To fetch her fan, her gloves, her mask, nor
nothing?

EMILIA

Never, my lord.

OTHELLO

That's strange.

EMILIA

I durst, my lord, to wager she is honest,
Lay down my soul at stake: if you think other,
Remove your thought; it doth abuse your
    bosom.
If any wretch have put this in your head,
Let heaven requite it with the serpent's curse!
For, if she be not honest, chaste, and true,
There's no man happy; the purest of their wives
Is foul as slander.

OTHELLO

Bid her come hither: go.

Exit EMILIA

She says enough; yet she's a simple bawd
That cannot say as much. This is a subtle whore,
A closet lock and key of villainous secrets
And yet she'll kneel and pray; I have seen her
    do't.

Enter DESDEMONA with EMILIA

DESDEMONA

My lord, what is your will?

OTHELLO

Pray, chuck, come hither.

DESDEMONA

What is your pleasure?

OTHELLO

Let me see your eyes;

Look in my face.

DESDEMONA

What horrible fancy's this?

OTHELLO

[*To EMILIA*] Some of your function, mistress;

Leave procreants alone and shut the door;

Cough, or cry 'hem,' if any body come:

Your mystery, your mystery: nay, dispatch.

Exit EMILIA

DESDEMONA

Upon my knees, what doth your speech import?

I understand a fury in your words.

But not the words.

OTHELLO

Why, what art thou?

DESDEMONA

Your wife, my lord; your true

And loyal wife.

OTHELLO

Come, swear it, damn thyself

Lest, being like one of heaven, the devils themselves

Should fear to seize thee: therefore be double damn'd:

Swear thou art honest.

DESDEMONA

Heaven doth truly know it.

OTHELLO

Heaven truly knows that thou art false as hell.

DESDEMONA

To whom, my lord? With whom? How am I false?

OTHELLO

O Desdemona! away! away! away!

DESDEMONA

Alas the heavy day! Why do you weep?

Am I the motive of these tears, my lord?

If haply you my father do suspect

An instrument of this your calling back,

Lay not your blame on me: If you have lost him,

Why, I have lost him too.

OTHELLO

Had it pleased heaven

To try me with affliction; had they rain'd

All kinds of sores and shames on my bare head.

Steep'd me in poverty to the very lips,

Given to captivity me and my utmost hopes,

I should have found in some place of my soul

A drop of patience: but, alas, to make me

A fixed figure for the time of scorn

To point his slow unmoving finger at!—O, O!

Yet could I bear that too; well, very well:
But there, where I have garner'd up my heart,
Where either I must live, or bear no life;
The fountain from the which my current runs,
Or else dries up; to be discarded thence!
Or keep it as a cistern for foul toads
To knot and gender in! Turn thy complexion
    there,
Patience, thou young and rose-lipp'd cherubin—
Ay, there, look grim as hell!

DESDEMONA

I hope my noble lord esteems me honest.

OTHELLO

O, ay; as summer flies are in the shambles,
That quicken even with blowing. O thou weed,
Who art so lovely fair and smell'st so sweet
That the sense aches at thee, would thou hadst
    ne'er been born!

DESDEMONA

Alas, what ignorant sin have I committed?

OTHELLO

Was this fair paper, this most goodly book,
Made to write 'whore' upon? What committed!
Committed! O thou public commoner!
I should make very forges of my cheeks,
That would to cinders burn up modesty,
Did I but speak thy deeds. What committed!

Heaven stops the nose at it and the moon winks,
The bawdy wind that kisses all it meets
Is hush'd within the hollow mine of earth,
And will not hear it. What committed!
Impudent strumpet!

DESDEMONA

By heaven, you do me wrong.

OTHELLO

Are you not a strumpet?

DESDEMONA

No, as I am a Christian:
If to preserve this vessel for my lord
From any other foul unlawful touch
Be not to be a strumpet, I am none.

OTHELLO

What, not a whore?

DESDEMONA

No, as I shall be saved.

OTHELLO

Is't possible?

DESDEMONA

O, heaven forgive us!

OTHELLO

I cry you mercy, then:
I took you for that cunning whore of Venice
That married with Othello.

Raising his voice

You, mistress,

That have the office opposite to Saint Peter,

And keep the gate of hell!

Re-enter EMILIA

You, you, ay, you!

We have done our course; there's money for
your pains:

I pray you, turn the key and keep our counsel.

Exit

EMILIA

Alas, what does this gentleman conceive?

How do you, madam? How do you, my good
lady?

DESDEMONA

'Faith, half asleep.

EMILIA

Good madam, what's the matter with my lord?

DESDEMONA

With who?

EMILIA

Why, with my lord, madam.

DESDEMONA

Who is thy lord?

EMILIA

He that is yours, sweet lady.

DESDEMONA

I have none: do not talk to me, Emilia;

I cannot weep; nor answer have I none,
But what should go by water. Prithee, tonight
Lay on my bed my wedding sheets: remember;
And call thy husband hither.

EMILIA

Here's a change indeed!

Exit

DESDEMONA

'Tis meet I should be used so, very meet.
How have I been behaved, that he might stick
The small'st opinion on my great'st abuse?

Re-enter EMILIA
with IAGO

IAGO

What is your pleasure, madam?
How is't with you?

DESDEMONA

I cannot tell. Those that do teach young babes
Do it with gentle means and easy tasks:
He might have chid me so; for, in good faith,
I am a child to chiding.

IAGO

What's the matter, lady?

EMILIA

Alas, Iago, my lord hath so bewhored her.
Thrown such despite and heavy terms upon her,
As true hearts cannot bear.

DESDEMONA

Am I that name, Iago?

IAGO

What name, fair lady?

DESDEMONA

Such as she says my lord did say I was.

EMILIA

He call'd her whore: a beggar in his drink
Could not have laid such terms upon his callat.

IAGO

Why did he so?

DESDEMONA

I do not know; I am sure I am none such.

IAGO

Do not weep, do not weep. Alas the day!

EMILIA

Hath she forsook so many noble matches,
Her father and her country and her friends,
To be call'd whore? Would it not make one weep?

DESDEMONA

It is my wretched fortune.

IAGO

Beshrew him for't!
How comes this trick upon him?

DESDEMONA

Nay, heaven doth know.

EMILIA

> I will be hang'd, if some eternal villain,
> Some busy and insinuating rogue,
> Some cogging, cozening slave, to get some office,
> Have not devised this slander; I'll be hang'd
>   else.

IAGO

> Fie, there is no such man; it is impossible.

DESDEMONA

> If any such there be, heaven pardon him!

EMILIA

> A halter pardon him! and hell gnaw his bones!
> Why should he call her whore? Who keeps her
>   company?
> What place? What time? What form? What
>   likelihood?
> The Moor's abused by some most villainous
>   knave,
> Some base notorious knave, some scurvy
>   fellow.
> O heaven, that such companions thou'ldst unfold,
> And put in every honest hand a whip
> To lash the rascals naked through the world
> Even from the east to the west!

IAGO

> Speak within door.

EMILIA

O, fie upon them! Some such squire he was
That turn'd your wit the seamy side without,
And made you to suspect me with the Moor.

IAGO

You are a fool; go to.

DESDEMONA

O good Iago,
What shall I do to win my lord again?
Good friend, go to him; for, by this light of
heaven,
I know not how I lost him. Here I kneel:
If e'er my will did trespass 'gainst his love,
Either in discourse of thought or actual deed,
Or that mine eyes, mine ears, or any sense,
Delighted them in any other form;
Or that I do not yet, and ever did.
And ever will—though he do shake me off
To beggarly divorcement—love him dearly,
Comfort forswear me! Unkindness may do much;
And his unkindness may defeat my life,
But never taint my love. I cannot say 'whore:'
It does abhor me now I speak the word;
To do the act that might the addition earn
Not the world's mass of vanity could make me.

IAGO

I pray you, be content; 'tis but his humour:

The business of the state does him offence,
And he does chide with you.

DESDEMONA

If 'twere no other—

IAGO

'Tis but so, I warrant.

Trumpets within

Hark, how these instruments summon you to
    supper!
The messengers of Venice stay the meat;
Go in, and weep not; all things shall be well.

Exeunt DESDEMONA and
EMILIA

Enter RODERIGO

How now, Roderigo!

RODERIGO

I do not find that thou dealest justly with me.

IAGO

What in the contrary?

RODERIGO

Every day thou daffest me with some device,
Iago; and rather, as it seems to me now, keepest
from me all conveniency than suppliest me
with the least advantage of hope. I will indeed
no longer endure it, nor am I yet persuaded to
put up in peace what already I have foolishly
suffered.

IAGO

Will you hear me, Roderigo?

RODERIGO

'Faith, I have heard too much, for your words and performances are no kin together.

IAGO

You charge me most unjustly.

RODERIGO

With nought but truth. I have wasted myself out of my means. The jewels you have had from me to deliver to Desdemona would half have corrupted a votarist: you have told me she hath received them and returned me expectations and comforts of sudden respect and acquaintance, but I find none.

IAGO

Well; go to; very well.

RODERIGO

Very well! go to! I cannot go to, man; nor 'tis not very well: by this hand, I say it is scurvy, and begin to find myself fobbed in it.

IAGO

Very well.

RODERIGO

I tell you 'tis not very well. I will make myself known to Desdemona: if she will return me my jewels, I will give over my suit and repent my

unlawful solicitation; if not, assure yourself I
will seek satisfaction of you.

IAGO

You have said now.

RODERIGO

Ay, and said nothing but what I protest
intendment of doing.

IAGO

Why, now I see there's mettle in thee, and
even from this instant to build on thee a better
opinion than ever before. Give me thy hand,
Roderigo: thou hast taken against me a most
just exception; but yet, I protest, I have dealt
most directly in thy affair.

RODERIGO

It hath not appeared.

IAGO

I grant indeed it hath not appeared, and your
suspicion is not without wit and judgment.
But, Roderigo, if thou hast that in thee indeed,
which I have greater reason to believe now than
ever, I mean purpose, courage and valour, this
night show it: if thou the next night following
enjoy not Desdemona, take me from this world
with treachery and devise engines for my life.

RODERIGO

Well, what is it? Is it within reason and compass?

IAGO

Sir, there is especial commission come from
Venice to depute Cassio in Othello's place.

RODERIGO

Is that true? Why, then Othello and Desdemona
return again to Venice.

IAGO

O, no; he goes into Mauritania and takes away
with him the fair Desdemona, unless his abode
be lingered here by some accident: wherein none
can be so determinate as the removing of Cassio.

RODERIGO

How do you mean, removing of him?

IAGO

Why, by making him uncapable of Othello's
place; knocking out his brains.

RODERIGO

And that you would have me to do?

IAGO

Ay, if you dare do yourself a profit and a
right. He sups to-night with a harlotry, and
thither will I go to him: he knows not yet of
his honourable fortune. If you will watch his
going thence, which I will fashion to fall out
between twelve and one, you may take him at
your pleasure: I will be near to second your
attempt, and he shall fall between us. Come,

stand not amazed at it, but go along with me;
I will show you such a necessity in his death
that you shall think yourself bound to put it on
him. It is now high suppertime, and the night
grows to waste: about it.

RODERIGO

I will hear further reason for this.

IAGO

And you shall be satisfied.

Exeunt

SCENE III. ANOTHER
ROOM IN THE CASTLE.

*Enter OTHELLO, LODOVICO, DESDEMONA,
EMILIA and Attendants*

LODOVICO

I do beseech you, sir, trouble yourself no further.

OTHELLO

O, pardon me: 'twill do me good to walk.

LODOVICO

Madam, good night; I humbly thank your
ladyship.

DESDEMONA

Your honour is most welcome.

OTHELLO

Will you walk, sir? O, Desdemona!

DESDEMONA

    My lord?

OTHELLO

    Get you to bed on the instant; I will be returned
    forthwith: dismiss your attendant there: look it
    be done.

DESDEMONA

    I will, my lord.

Exeunt OTHELLO,
LODOVICO, and Attendants

EMILIA

    How goes it now? He looks gentler than he did.

DESDEMONA

    He says he will return incontinent:
    He hath commanded me to go to bed,
    And bade me to dismiss you.

EMILIA

    Dismiss me!

DESDEMONA

    It was his bidding: therefore, good Emilia,
    Give me my nightly wearing, and adieu:
    We must not now displease him.

EMILIA

    I would you had never seen him!

DESDEMONA

    So would not I my love doth so approve him,

That even his stubbornness, his checks, his
    frowns—

Prithee, unpin me—have grace and favour in
    them.

EMILIA

I have laid those sheets you bade me on the bed.

DESDEMONA

All's one. Good faith, how foolish are our minds!

If I do die before thee prithee, shroud me

In one of those same sheets.

EMILIA

Come, come you talk.

DESDEMONA

My mother had a maid call'd Barbara:

She was in love, and he she loved proved mad

And did forsake her: she had a song of 'willow;'

An old thing 'twas, but it express'd her fortune,

And she died singing it: that song to-night

Will not go from my mind; I have much to do,

But to go hang my head all at one side,

And sing it like poor Barbara. Prithee, dispatch.

EMILIA

Shall I go fetch your night-gown?

DESDEMONA

No, unpin me here.

This Lodovico is a proper man.

EMILIA

A very handsome man.

DESDEMONA

He speaks well.

EMILIA

I know a lady in Venice would have walked
barefoot to Palestine for a touch of his nether lip.

DESDEMONA

[*Singing*] The poor soul sat sighing by a sycamore
tree, Sing all a green willow:

Her hand on her bosom, her head on her knee,
Sing willow, willow, willow:

The fresh streams ran by her, and murmur'd
her moans; Sing willow, willow, willow;

Her salt tears fell from her, and soften'd the stones;

Lay by these:—

Sing willow, willow, willow;

Prithee, hie thee; he'll come anon:—

Sing all a green willow must be my garland.

Let nobody blame him; his scorn I approve—

Nay, that's not next. Hark! who is't that knocks?

EMILIA

It's the wind.

DESDEMONA

[*Singing*] I call'd my love false love; but what said
he then?

Sing willow, willow, willow:

If I court moe women, you'll couch with moe
    men!

So, get thee gone; good night Mine eyes do itch;
Doth that bode weeping?

EMILIA

'Tis neither here nor there.

DESDEMONA

I have heard it said so. O, these men, these men!
Dost thou in conscience think—tell me, Emilia—
That there be women do abuse their husbands
In such gross kind?

EMILIA

There be some such, no question.

DESDEMONA

Wouldst thou do such a deed for all the world?

EMILIA

Why, would not you?

DESDEMONA

No, by this heavenly light!

EMILIA

Nor I neither by this heavenly light;
I might do't as well i' the dark.

DESDEMONA

Wouldst thou do such a deed for all the world?

EMILIA

The world's a huge thing: it is a great price.
For a small vice.

DESDEMONA

In troth, I think thou wouldst not.

EMILIA

In troth, I think I should; and undo't when I had done. Marry, I would not do such a thing for a joint-ring, nor for measures of lawn, nor for gowns, petticoats, nor caps, nor any petty exhibition; but for the whole world—why, who would not make her husband a cuckold to make him a monarch? I should venture purgatory for't.

DESDEMONA

Beshrew me, if I would do such a wrong for the whole world.

EMILIA

Why the wrong is but a wrong i' the world: and having the world for your labour, tis a wrong in your own world, and you might quickly make it right.

DESDEMONA

I do not think there is any such woman.

EMILIA

Yes, a dozen; and as many to the vantage as
    would store the world they played for.
But I do think it is their husbands' faults
If wives do fall: say that they slack their duties,
And pour our treasures into foreign laps,

Or else break out in peevish jealousies,
Throwing restraint upon us; or say they strike us,
Or scant our former having in despite;
Why, we have galls, and though we have some
    grace,
Yet have we some revenge. Let husbands know
Their wives have sense like them: they see and
    smell
And have their palates both for sweet and sour,
As husbands have. What is it that they do
When they change us for others? Is it sport?
I think it is: and doth affection breed it?
I think it doth: is't frailty that thus errs?
It is so too: and have not we affections,
Desires for sport, and frailty, as men have?
Then let them use us well: else let them know,
The ills we do, their ills instruct us so.

DESDEMONA

    Good night, good night: heaven me such uses
        send,
    Not to pick bad from bad, but by bad mend!

                              Exeunt

Act V

SCENE I. CYPRUS. A STREET.

Enter IAGO and RODERIGO

IAGO

    Here, stand behind this bulk; straight will he
        come:

    Wear thy good rapier bare, and put it home:

    Quick, quick; fear nothing; I'll be at thy elbow:

    It makes us, or it mars us; think on that,

    And fix most firm thy resolution.

RODERIGO

    Be near at hand; I may miscarry in't.

IAGO

    Here, at thy hand: be bold, and take thy stand.

                    Retires

RODERIGO

    I have no great devotion to the deed;

And yet he hath given me satisfying reasons:
'Tis but a man gone. Forth, my sword: he dies.

IAGO

I have rubb'd this young quat almost to the
    sense,
And he grows angry. Now, whether he kill
    Cassio,
Or Cassio him, or each do kill the other,
Every way makes my gain: live Roderigo,
He calls me to a restitution large
Of gold and jewels that I bobb'd from him,
As gifts to Desdemona;
It must not be: if Cassio do remain,
He hath a daily beauty in his life
That makes me ugly; and, besides, the Moor
May unfold me to him; there stand I in much
    peril:
No, he must die. But so: I hear him coming.

Enter CASSIO

RODERIGO

I know his gait, 'tis he. Villain, thou diest!

Makes a pass at CASSIO

CASSIO

That thrust had been mine enemy indeed,
But that my coat is better than thou know'st
I will make proof of thine.

Draws, and wounds RODERIGO

RODERIGO

O, I am slain!

IAGO from behind wounds
CASSIO in the leg, and exit

CASSIO

I am maim'd for ever. Help, ho! murder!
murder!
Falls

Enter OTHELLO

OTHELLO

The voice of Cassio: Iago keeps his word.

RODERIGO

O, villain that I am!

OTHELLO

It is even so.

CASSIO

O, help, ho! light! a surgeon!

OTHELLO

'Tis he:—O brave Iago, honest and just,
That hast such noble sense of thy friend's wrong!
Thou teachest me. Minion, your dear lies dead,
And your unblest fate hies: strumpet, I come.
Forth of my heart those charms, thine eyes, are
blotted;
Thy bed, lust-stain'd, shall with lust's blood be
spotted.

Exit

Enter LODOVICO and GRATIANO

CASSIO

What, ho! no watch? No passage? Murder! murder!

GRATIANO

'Tis some mischance; the cry is very direful.

CASSIO

O, help!

LODOVICO

Hark!

RODERIGO

O wretched villain!

LODOVICO

Two or three groan: it is a heavy night:

These may be counterfeits: let's think't unsafe

To come in to the cry without more help.

RODERIGO

Nobody come? Then shall I bleed to death.

LODOVICO

Hark!

Re-enter IAGO, with a light

GRATIANO

Here's one comes in his shirt, with light and weapons.

IAGO

Who's there? Whose noise is this that ones on murder?

LODOVICO

We do not know.

IAGO

Did not you hear a cry?

CASSIO

Here, here! for heaven's sake, help me!

IAGO

What's the matter?

GRATIANO

This is Othello's ancient, as I take it.

LODOVICO

The same indeed; a very valiant fellow.

IAGO

What are you here that cry so grievously?

CASSIO

Iago? O, I am spoil'd, undone by villains!

Give me some help.

IAGO

O me, lieutenant! what villains have done this?

CASSIO

I think that one of them is hereabout,

And cannot make away.

IAGO

O treacherous villains!

What are you there? Come in, and give some

help.

To LODOVICO and GRATIANO

RODERIGO

O, help me here!

CASSIO

That's one of them.

IAGO

O murderous slave! O villain!

Stabs RODERIGO

RODERIGO

O damn'd Iago! O inhuman dog!

IAGO

Kill men i' the dark! Where be these bloody
thieves?

How silent is this town! Ho! murder! murder!

What may you be? Are you of good or evil?

LODOVICO

As you shall prove us, praise us.

IAGO

Signior Lodovico?

LODOVICO

He, sir.

IAGO

I cry you mercy. Here's Cassio hurt by villains.

GRATIANO

Cassio!

IAGO

How is't, brother!

CASSIO

My leg is cut in two.

IAGO

Marry, heaven forbid!

Light, gentlemen; I'll bind it with my shirt.

Enter BIANCA

BIANCA

What is the matter, ho? Who is't that cried?

IAGO

Who is't that cried!

BIANCA

O my dear Cassio! my sweet Cassio! O Cassio,
Cassio, Cassio!

IAGO

O notable strumpet! Cassio, may you suspect
Who they should be that have thus many led
    you?

CASSIO

No.

GRATIANO

I am to find you thus: I have been to seek you.

IAGO

Lend me a garter. So. O, for a chair,
To bear him easily hence!

BIANCA

Alas, he faints! O Cassio, Cassio, Cassio!

IAGO

    Gentlemen all, I do suspect this trash
    To be a party in this injury.
    Patience awhile, good Cassio. Come, come;
    Lend me a light. Know we this face or no?
    Alas my friend and my dear countryman
    Roderigo! no:—yes, sure: O heaven! Roderigo.

GRATIANO

    What, of Venice?

IAGO

    Even he, sir; did you know him?

GRATIANO

    Know him! ay.

IAGO

    Signior Gratiano? I cry you gentle pardon;
    These bloody accidents must excuse my
        manners,
    That so neglected you.

GRATIANO

    I am glad to see you.

IAGO

    How do you, Cassio? O, a chair, a chair!

GRATIANO

    Roderigo!

IAGO

    He, he 'tis he.

               A chair brought in

O, that's well said; the chair!

Some good man bear him carefully from hence;

I'll fetch the general's surgeon.

To BIANCA

For you, mistress,

Save you your labour. He that lies slain here,
    Cassio,

Was my dear friend: what malice was between
    you?

CASSIO

None in the world; nor do I know the man.

IAGO

[*To BIANCA*] What, look you pale? O, bear
him out o' the air.

CASSIO and RODERIGO are borne off

Stay you, good gentlemen. Look you pale,
    mistress?

Do you perceive the gastness of her eye?

Nay, if you stare, we shall hear more anon.

Behold her well; I pray you, look upon her:

Do you see, gentlemen? Nay, guiltiness will
    speak,

Though tongues were out of use.

Enter EMILIA

EMILIA

'Las, what's the matter? What's the matter,
husband?

IAGO

    Cassio hath here been set on in the dark

    By Roderigo and fellows that are scaped:

    He's almost slain, and Roderigo dead.

EMILIA

    Alas, good gentleman! alas, good Cassio!

IAGO

    This is the fruit of whoring. Prithee, Emilia,

    Go know of Cassio where he supp'd to-night.

                To BIANCA

    What, do you shake at that?

BIANCA

    He supp'd at my house; but I therefore shake
    not.

IAGO

    O, did he so? I charge you, go with me.

EMILIA

    Fie, fie upon thee, strumpet!

BIANCA

    I am no strumpet; but of life as honest

    As you that thus abuse me.

EMILIA

    As I! foh! fie upon thee!

IAGO

    Kind gentlemen, let's go see poor Cassio dress'd.

    Come, mistress, you must tell's another tale.

    Emilia run you to the citadel,

And tell my lord and lady what hath happ'd.
Will you go on? I pray.
Aside
This is the night
That either makes me or fordoes me quite.

Exeunt

SCENE II. A BEDCHAMBER IN THE CASTLE.

DESDEMONA in bed asleep; a light burning.
Enter OTHELLO
OTHELLO

It is the cause, it is the cause, my soul—
Let me not name it to you, you chaste stars—
It is the cause. Yet I'll not shed her blood;
Nor scar that whiter skin of hers than snow,
And smooth as monumental alabaster.
Yet she must die, else she'll betray more men.
Put out the light, and then put out the light:
If I quench thee, thou flaming minister,
I can again thy former light restore,
Should I repent me: but once put out thy light,
Thou cunning'st pattern of excelling nature,
I know not where is that Promethean heat
That can thy light relume. When I have pluck'd
the rose,

I cannot give it vital growth again.
It must needs wither: I'll smell it on the tree.

Kissing her

Ah balmy breath, that dost almost persuade
Justice to break her sword! One more, one
more.
Be thus when thou art dead, and I will kill thee,
And love thee after. One more, and this the last:
So sweet was ne'er so fatal. I must weep,
But they are cruel tears: this sorrow's heavenly;
It strikes where it doth love. She wakes.

DESDEMONA

Who's there? Othello?

OTHELLO

Ay. Desdemona.

DESDEMONA

Will you come to bed, my lord?

OTHELLO

Have you pray'd to-night, Desdemona?

DESDEMONA

Ay, my lord.

OTHELLO

If you bethink yourself of any crime
Unreconciled as yet to heaven and grace,
Solicit for it straight.

DESDEMONA

Alas, my lord, what do you mean by that?

OTHELLO

Well, do it, and be brief; I will walk by:

I would not kill thy unprepared spirit;

No; heaven forfend! I would not kill thy soul.

DESDEMONA

Talk you of killing?

OTHELLO

Ay, I do.

DESDEMONA

Then heaven

Have mercy on me!

OTHELLO

Amen, with all my heart!

DESDEMONA

If you say so, I hope you will not kill me.

OTHELLO

Hum!

DESDEMONA

And yet I fear you; for you are fatal then

When your eyes roll so: why I should fear I
    know not,

Since guiltiness I know not; but yet I feel I fear.

OTHELLO

Think on thy sins.

DESDEMONA

They are loves I bear to you.

OTHELLO

Ay, and for that thou diest.

DESDEMONA

That death's unnatural that kills for loving.
Alas, why gnaw you so your nether lip?
Some bloody passion shakes your very frame:
These are portents; but yet I hope, I hope,
They do not point on me.

OTHELLO

Peace, and be still!

DESDEMONA

I will so. What's the matter?

OTHELLO

That handkerchief which I so loved and gave
thee
Thou gavest to Cassio.

DESDEMONA

No, by my life and soul!
Send for the man, and ask him.

OTHELLO

Sweet soul, take heed,
Take heed of perjury; thou art on thy deathbed.

DESDEMONA

Ay, but not yet to die.

OTHELLO

Yes, presently:
Therefore confess thee freely of thy sin;

For to deny each article with oath
Cannot remove nor choke the strong
    conception
That I do groan withal. Thou art to die.

DESDEMONA

Then Lord have mercy on me!

OTHELLO

I say, amen.

DESDEMONA

And have you mercy too! I never did
Offend you in my life; never loved Cassio
But with such general warranty of heaven
As I might love: I never gave him token.

OTHELLO

By heaven, I saw my handkerchief in's hand.
O perjured woman! thou dost stone my heart,
And makest me call what I intend to do
A murder, which I thought a sacrifice:
I saw the handkerchief.

DESDEMONA

He found it then;
I never gave it him: send for him hither;
Let him confess a truth.

OTHELLO

He hath confess'd.

DESDEMONA

What, my lord?

OTHELLO

That he hath used thee.

DESDEMONA

How? unlawfully?

OTHELLO

Ay.

DESDEMONA

He will not say so.

OTHELLO

No, his mouth is stopp'd;

Honest Iago hath ta'en order for't.

DESDEMONA

O! my fear interprets: what, is he dead?

OTHELLO

Had all his hairs been lives, my great revenge

Had stomach for them all.

DESDEMONA

Alas! he is betray'd and I undone.

OTHELLO

Out, strumpet! weep'st thou for him to my face?

DESDEMONA

O, banish me, my lord, but kill me not!

OTHELLO

Down, strumpet!

DESDEMONA

Kill me to-morrow: let me live to-night!

OTHELLO

Nay, if you strive—

DESDEMONA

But half an hour!

OTHELLO

Being done, there is no pause.

DESDEMONA

But while I say one prayer!

OTHELLO

It is too late.

He stifles her

DESDEMONA

O lord, Lord, Lord!

EMILIA

[*Within*] My lord , my lord! what, ho! my lord, my lord!

OTHELLO

What noise is this? Not dead? not yet quite dead?

I that am cruel am yet merciful;

I would not have thee linger in thy pain: So, so.

EMILIA

[*Within*] What, ho! my lord, my lord!

OTHELLO

Who's there?

EMILIA

[*Within*] O, good my lord, I would speak a word with you!

OTHELLO

Yes: 'tis Emilia. By and by. She's dead.
'Tis like she comes to speak of Cassio's death—
The noise was here. Ha! no more moving?
Still as the grave. Shall she come in? Were't
    good?
I think she stirs again:—no. What's best to do?
If she come in, she'll sure speak to my wife:
My wife! my wife! what wife? I have no wife.
O insupportable! O heavy hour!
Methinks it should be now a huge eclipse
Of sun and moon, and that the affrighted globe
Should yawn at alteration.

EMILIA

[*Within*] I do beseech you
That I may speak with you, O, good my lord!

OTHELLO

I had forgot thee: O, come in, Emilia;
Soft; by and by. Let me the curtains draw.
Where art thou?

> *Unlocks the door*
> *Enter EMILIA*

What's the matter with thee now?

EMILIA

O, my good lord, yonder's foul murders done!

OTHELLO

What, now?

EMILIA

But now, my lord.

OTHELLO

It is the very error of the moon;

She comes more nearer earth than she was wont,

And makes men mad.

EMILIA

Cassio, my lord, hath kill'd a young Venetian

Call'd Roderigo.

OTHELLO

Roderigo kill'd!

And Cassio kill'd!

EMILIA

No, Cassio is not kill'd.

OTHELLO

Not Cassio kill'd! then murder's out of tune,

And sweet revenge grows harsh.

DESDEMONA

O, falsely, falsely murder'd!

EMILIA

Alas, what cry is that?

OTHELLO

That! what?

EMILIA

Out, and alas! that was my lady's voice.

Help! help, ho! help! O lady, speak again!

Sweet Desdemona! O sweet mistress, speak!

DESDEMONA

A guiltless death I die.

EMILIA

O, who hath done this deed?

DESDEMONA

Nobody; I myself. Farewell

Commend me to my kind lord: O, farewell!

She dies

OTHELLO

Why, how should she be murder'd?

EMILIA

Alas, who knows?

OTHELLO

You heard her say herself, it was not I.

EMILIA

She said so: I must needs report the truth.

OTHELLO

She's, like a liar, gone to burning hell:

'Twas I that kill'd her.

EMILIA

O, the more angel she,

And you the blacker devil!

OTHELLO

She turn'd to folly, and she was a whore.

EMILIA

Thou dost belie her, and thou art a devil.

OTHELLO

She was false as water.

EMILIA

Thou art rash as fire, to say

That she was false: O, she was heavenly true!

OTHELLO

Cassio did top her; ask thy husband else.

O, I were damn'd beneath all depth in hell,

But that I did proceed upon just grounds

To this extremity. Thy husband knew it all.

EMILIA

My husband!

OTHELLO

Thy husband.

EMILIA

That she was false to wedlock?

OTHELLO

Ay, with Cassio. Nay, had she been true,

If heaven would make me such another world

Of one entire and Perfect chrysolite,

I'ld not have sold her for it.

EMILIA

My husband!

OTHELLO

Ay, 'twas he that told me first:

An honest man he is, and hates the slime

That sticks on filthy deeds.

EMILIA

My husband!

OTHELLO

What needs this iteration, woman? I say thy
husband.

EMILIA

O mistress, villainy hath made mocks with love,
My husband say that she was false!

OTHELLO

He, woman;
I say thy husband: dost understand the word?
My friend, thy husband, honest, honest Iago.

EMILIA

If he say so, may his pernicious soul
Rot half a grain a day! he lies to the heart:
She was too fond of her most filthy bargain.

OTHELLO

Ha!

EMILIA

Do thy worst:
This deed of thine is no more worthy heaven
Than thou wast worthy her.

OTHELLO

Peace, you were best.

EMILIA

Thou hast not half that power to do me harm
As I have to be hurt. O gull! O dolt!

As ignorant as dirt! thou hast done a deed—
I care not for thy sword; I'll make thee known,
Though I lost twenty lives. Help! help, ho! help!
The Moor hath kill'd my mistress! Murder!
 murder!

 Enter MONTANO, GRATIANO,
   IAGO, and others

MONTANO
 What is the matter? How now, general!

EMILIA
 O, are you come, Iago? you have done well,
 That men must lay their murders on your neck.

GRATIANO
 What is the matter?

EMILIA
 Disprove this villain, if thou be'st a man:
 He says thou told'st him that his wife was false:
 I know thou didst not, thou'rt not such a villain:
 Speak, for my heart is full.

IAGO
 I told him what I thought, and told no more
 Than what he found himself was apt and true.

EMILIA
 But did you ever tell him she was false?

IAGO
 I did.

EMILIA

You told a lie, an odious, damned lie;

Upon my soul, a lie, a wicked lie.

She false with Cassio! did you say with Cassio?

IAGO

With Cassio, mistress. Go to, charm your tongue.

EMILIA

I will not charm my tongue; I am bound to
speak:

My mistress here lies murder'd in her bed—

ALL

O heavens forfend!

EMILIA

And your reports have set the murder on.

OTHELLO

Nay, stare not, masters: it is true, indeed.

GRATIANO

'Tis a strange truth.

MONTANO

O monstrous act!

EMILIA

Villainy, villainy, villainy!

I think upon't, I think: I smell't: O villainy!

I thought so then:—I'll kill myself for grief:—

O villainy, villainy!

IAGO

What, are you mad? I charge you, get you home.

EMILIA

Good gentlemen, let me have leave to speak:

'Tis proper I obey him, but not now.

Perchance, Iago, I will ne'er go home.

OTHELLO

O! O! O!

He falls on the bed

EMILIA

Nay, lay thee down and roar;

For thou hast kill'd the sweetest innocent

That e'er did lift up eye.

OTHELLO

[*Rising*] O, she was foul!

I scarce did know you, uncle: there lies your niece,

Whose breath, indeed, these hands have newly stopp'd:

I know this act shows horrible and grim.

GRATIANO

Poor Desdemona! I am glad thy father's dead:

Thy match was mortal to him, and pure grief

Shore his old thread in twain: did he live now,

This sight would make him do a desperate turn,

Yea, curse his better angel from his side,

And fall to reprobation.

OTHELLO

'Tis pitiful; but yet Iago knows

That she with Cassio hath the act of shame
A thousand times committed; Cassio confess'd it:
And she did gratify his amorous works
With that recognizance and pledge of love
Which I first gave her; I saw it in his hand:
It was a handkerchief, an antique token
My father gave my mother.

EMILIA

O heaven! O heavenly powers!

IAGO

Come, hold your peace.

EMILIA

'Twill out, 'twill out: I peace!
No, I will speak as liberal as the north:
Let heaven and men and devils, let them all,
All, all, cry shame against me, yet I'll speak.

IAGO

Be wise, and get you home.

EMILIA

I will not.

   IAGO offers to stab EMILIA

GRATIANO

Fie!
Your sword upon a woman?

EMILIA

O thou dull Moor! that handkerchief thou
 speak'st of

I found by fortune and did give my husband;
For often, with a solemn earnestness,
More than indeed belong'd to such a trifle,
He begg'd of me to steal it.

IAGO

Villainous whore!

EMILIA

She give it Cassio! no, alas! I found it,
And I did give't my husband.

IAGO

Filth, thou liest!

EMILIA

By heaven, I do not, I do not, gentlemen.
O murderous coxcomb! what should such a fool
Do with so good a woman?

OTHELLO

Are there no stones in heaven
But what serve for the thunder? Precious villain!
*He runs at IAGO; MONTANO and
others disarm him. IAGO, from behind,
stabs EMILIA, and escapes*

GRATIANO

The woman falls; sure, he hath kill'd his wife.

EMILIA

Ay, ay: O, lay me by my mistress' side.

GRATIANO

He's gone, but his wife's kill'd.

MONTANO

'Tis a notorious villain. Take you this weapon,
Which I have here recover'd from the Moor:
Come, guard the door without; let him not pass,
But kill him rather. I'll after that same villain,
For 'tis a damned slave.

Exeunt MONTANO and
GRATIANO and other

OTHELLO

I am not valiant neither,
But ever puny whipster gets my sword:
But why should honour outlive honesty?
Let it go all.

EMILIA

What did thy song bode, lady?
Hark, canst thou hear me? I will play the swan.
And die in music.

Singing

Willow, willow, willow—

Moor, she was chaste; she loved thee, cruel Moor;
So come my soul to bliss, as I speak true;
So speaking as I think, I die, I die.

She dies

OTHELLO

I have another weapon in this chamber;
It is a sword of Spain, the ice-brook's temper:—
O, here it is. Uncle, I must come forth.

GRATIANO

[*Within*] If thou attempt it, it will cost thee dear:
Thou hast no weapon, and perforce must
    suffer.

OTHELLO

Look in upon me then and speak with me,
Or, naked as I am, I will assault thee.

Re-enter GRATIANO

GRATIANO

What is the matter?

OTHELLO

Behold, I have a weapon;
A better never did itself sustain
Upon a soldier's thigh: I have seen the day,
That, with this little arm and this good sword,
I have made my way through more impediments
Than twenty times your stop: but, O vain boast!
Who can control his fate? 'Tis not so now.
Be not afraid, though you do see me weapon'd;
Here is my journey's end, here is my butt,
And very sea-mark of my utmost sail.
Do you go back dismay'd? 'Tis a lost fear;
Man but a rush against Othello's breast,
And he retires. Where should Othello go?
Now, how dost thou look now? O ill-starr'd
    wench!
Pale as thy smock! when we shall meet at compt,

This look of thine will hurl my soul from
    heaven,
And fiends will snatch at it. Cold, cold, my girl!
Even like thy chastity. O cursed slave!
Whip me, ye devils,
From the possession of this heavenly sight!
Blow me about in winds! roast me in sulphur!
Wash me in steep-down gulfs of liquid fire!
O Desdemona! Desdemona! dead!
Oh! Oh! Oh!

    Enter LODOVICO. MONTANO,
      CASSIO carried in a chair, and
       Officers with IAGO, prisoner

LODOVICO

Where is this rash and most unfortunate man?

OTHELLO

That's he that was Othello: here I am.

LODOVICO

Where is that viper? Bring the villain forth.

OTHELLO

I look down towards his feet; but that's a fable.
If that thou best a devil, I cannot kill thee.

      Wounds IAGO

LODOVICO

Wrench his sword from him.

IAGO

I bleed, sir; but not kill'd.

OTHELLO

I am not sorry neither: I'ld have thee live;

For, in my sense, 'tis happiness to die.

LODOVICO

O thou Othello, thou wert once so good,

Fall'n in the practise of a damned slave,

What shall be said to thee?

OTHELLO

Why, any thing:

An honourable murderer, if you will;

For nought I did in hate, but all in honour.

LODOVICO

This wretch hath part confess'd his villany:

Did you and he consent in Cassio's death?

OTHELLO

Ay.

CASSIO

Dear general, I never gave you cause.

OTHELLO

I do believe it, and I ask your pardon.

Will you, I pray, demand that demi-devil

Why he hath thus ensnared my soul and body?

IAGO

Demand me nothing: what you know, you know:

From this time forth I never will speak word.

LODOVICO

What, not to pray?

GRATIANO

Torments will ope your lips.

OTHELLO

Well, thou dost best.

LODOVICO

Sir, you shall understand what hath befall'n,
Which, as I think, you know not. Here is a letter
Found in the pocket of the slain Roderigo;
And here another: the one of them imports
The death of Cassio to be undertook
By Roderigo.

OTHELLO

O villain!

CASSIO

Most heathenish and most gross!

LODOVICO

Now here's another discontented paper,
Found in his pocket too; and this, it seems,
Roderigo meant to have sent this damned
    villain;
But that belike Iago in the nick
Came in and satisfied him.

OTHELLO

O the pernicious caitiff!
How came you, Cassio, by that handkerchief
That was my wife's?

CASSIO

    I found it in my chamber:
    And he himself confess'd it even now
    That there he dropp'd it for a special purpose
    Which wrought to his desire.

OTHELLO

    O fool! fool! fool!

CASSIO

    There is besides in Roderigo's letter,
    How he upbraids Iago, that he made him
    Brave me upon the watch; whereon it came
    That I was cast: and even but now he spake,
    After long seeming dead, Iago hurt him,
    Iago set him on.

LODOVICO

    You must forsake this room, and go with us:
    Your power and your command is taken off,
    And Cassio rules in Cyprus. For this slave,
    If there be any cunning cruelty
    That can torment him much and hold him long,
    It shall be his. You shall close prisoner rest,
    Till that the nature of your fault be known
    To the Venetian state. Come, bring him away.

OTHELLO

    Soft you; a word or two before you go.
    I have done the state some service, and they
        know't.

No more of that. I pray you, in your letters,
When you shall these unlucky deeds relate,
Speak of me as I am; nothing extenuate,
Nor set down aught in malice: then must you
    speak
Of one that loved not wisely but too well;
Of one not easily jealous, but being wrought
Perplex'd in the extreme; of one whose hand,
Like the base Indian, threw a pearl away
Richer than all his tribe; of one whose subdued
    eyes,
Albeit unused to the melting mood,
Drop tears as fast as the Arabian trees
Their medicinal gum. Set you down this;
And say besides, that in Aleppo once,
Where a malignant and a turban'd Turk
Beat a Venetian and traduced the state,
I took by the throat the circumcised dog,
And smote him, thus.

Stabs himself

LODOVICO

O bloody period!

GRATIANO

All that's spoke is marr'd.

OTHELLO

I kiss'd thee ere I kill'd thee: no way but this;
Killing myself, to die upon a kiss.

Falls on the bed, and dies

CASSIO

This did I fear, but thought he had no weapon;
For he was great of heart.

LODOVICO

[*To IAGO*] O Spartan dog,
More fell than anguish, hunger, or the sea!
Look on the tragic loading of this bed;
This is thy work: the object poisons sight;
Let it be hid. Gratiano, keep the house,
And seize upon the fortunes of the Moor,
For they succeed on you. To you, lord governor,
Remains the censure of this hellish villain;
The time, the place, the torture: O, enforce it!
Myself will straight aboard: and to the state
This heavy act with heavy heart relate.

Exeunt